CYANIDE & HAPPINESS™

A GUIDE TO PARENTING BY THREE GUYS WITH NO KIDS

Comics by Kris, Rob and Dave
with Advice by Dave McElfatrick

BOOM!
STUDIOS

Table of Contents

Foreword

My son was a terrible sleeper. When he was a baby he used to wake up every 45 minutes screaming, which in turn woke my wife and I up. Bleary eyed and grumpy, one of us would stumble into his room and try everything we could to get him to be quiet. We would rock him gently and we would rock him hard (not shake though...never shake). We would turn him at different angles and walk him at different speeds. One night I discovered I could get him to stop crying if I walked up the stairs backwards holding him sideways. Thinking I had cracked the code I tried this same thing again the following evening. No luck. He just cried and cried and cried.

There is no happy ending to this story because there is no happy ending to living with children. Just a whole lot of pain and aggravation with some beautiful, touching moments sprinkled in. The people who make it through this journey alive are the ones who develop a strong sense of humor because if you don't learn to laugh at the fucked up journey that is parenting you will lose your mind.

If you are a parent reading this book then you have taken the right first step to becoming the kind of parent who will survive. Instead of buying that bullshit parenting book that claims to have all the answers, you have decided to spend your money on something that will make you laugh. If you aren't a parent and you are buying this book, then you have either lucked into the best find of the century or you already know that the boys behind *Cyanide and Happiness* do not disappoint.

For what feels like decades, *Cyanide and Happiness* has made us laugh, cringe, and think to ourselves, "Should I be laughing at this?" The answer is yes. Because although the authors of this book may not have ever witnessed the miracle of childbirth or perhaps ever even interacted with a child, they know that in order to survive this crazy weird life we need to keep laughing.

Chris Grady
Author of *Lunarbaboon*

Introduction

I tend to skip this part of books, so I'll keep it brief. I consider this part of the book akin to the ticket booth of a theme park, so you definitely won't catch me prattling on right here, holding you back from your fun. Not I.

Good evening. Or afternoon. Or morning, early or late. It's difficult for me to take a proper stab at the time you're reading this, as you're reading this at a dramatically different time from when I wrote it. Which to me is now, but to you it's also now, which is in the future for me, so in a way I am talking to a future version of you from right now, like a sort of clock wizard.

Perhaps you've been gifted this book by your child as a plea to treat them better, or maybe you've rushed into the bookstore in need of quick parenting advice after committing a clumsy act upon your child, like shaving the words "hot piss" into their hair. Heck, maybe you aren't even a parent, but you've been thinking about getting into it in the same way you'd like to try building a kite, or a luge. Either way, here you are, right now, holding your new book with smiling dinghy lips.

It is my immediate duty to disclose to you that I am not a parent, and barely a human being. This book is a conglomeration of information gained from years of eavesdropping, watching *Kindergarten Cop*, and pearls of wisdom passed to me from my own father before he left when I was 9. This information is arranged in no particular order, so I recommend casually diving in somewhere in the middle and working outwards from there. Though I have written this from the perspective of fatherhood as I am unimaginative and have a dick and balls, all wisdom within this book can equally apply to the joys of being a mother. Just switch genders as you read, like a clownfish.

To begin, please refer to the quick setup guide in the following section.

Quick Setup Guide

Follow this easy three-step guide to get your parenting setup running in no time:

YOU.

Fig. 1

Step A

The first ingredient on the list is you (see **Fig. 1**). Yes, you. We'll need all of you here. An entire serving. We'll need you to be of age—though it varies by state or country, you'll need to be around 16-18. Got that? Alright, you're halfway there already. Good job. Forget about your marbles. You won't necessarily need those. Any idiot can do this.

Step B

Okay, now that we've got you, the next step is to acquire another person with whom to make a child—after all, it takes two to tango, and two to fuck. If you already have another half, or spouse, then skip to **Step C**. If not, read on.

This is by far the easiest step. Simply approach another human being—perhaps in a public setting, such as a restaurant or speedboat—and ask them if they would like to make a baby with you. Be liberal with your askings. Ask multiple people at the restaurant, or cram multiple people onto what is presumably your speedboat. If you've done this correctly, you should have garnered a number of "absolutely, yes" responses, through which you can scour like a fisherman looking through his trawler net.

Depending on who you've hooked, you can move forward with varying degrees of difficulty. Let's run through your catch.

Fig. 2

Fig. 2 is a common option when selecting a mate with whom to conceive a child. Relatively expensive to maintain but mostly reliable, like a Mini Cooper. Has a two-door trunk as well. Like a Mini Cooper.

Fig. 3

Though it's unlikely that you'll be able to conceive a child with **Fig. 3**, you can certainly try. Absolutely try, in all sorts of different ways. Try often. I'm not stopping you. Who knows, perhaps if you keep trying, you'll come across a miracle—and I'm not talking about some dude called Miracle.

Fig. 4

Nope.

Step C

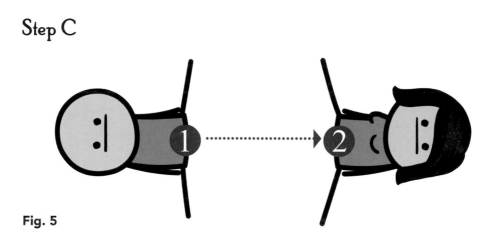

Fig. 5

Once you've found a reasonable mate, or host, now you must perform the act of creating a baby (**Fig. 5**). The only major step is to insert your pee pee (1) into her boomshakala (2), scientifically known as the hoochamama. Anything else is optional. You may derive pleasure from this part of the drill, but it is definitely not encouraged. Keep your mind on task.

The fiduciaries of intercourse can often prove clumsy and problematic, similar to trying to plug something into a power socket that's really far behind the couch. Depending on the utilities available to you, you may be able to reach with relative ease, or you may suffer defeat in a humiliating, confidence-destroying fashion. Here are some common positions you can use to help secure victory.

This is the industry standard of conception: old-fashioned and reliable. Use this if you want to stare soullessly into the face of the person you are invading.

Fig. 6

Fig. 7

Consider this option the "choose your own adventure" of intercourse. There is a fork in the road, and the direction you choose to take has severe consequences. Down one path, you will find companionship, parentage, and a sparkling new life of domesticity ahead of you. The other path leads to a potential mini-second of hedonism followed by a probable lifetime of disdain. Choose wisely. Treat the decision carefully, like which wire to cut when defusing a bomb.

If you've made the right decision, your partner will let you know. Now you can let loose. You are both now connected together like a train—you the carriage, your partner the thundering locomotive. Make pneumatic motions with your arms, and be a choo-choo train. Beep if you like. Enjoy yourself.

Fig. 8

Just try this one.

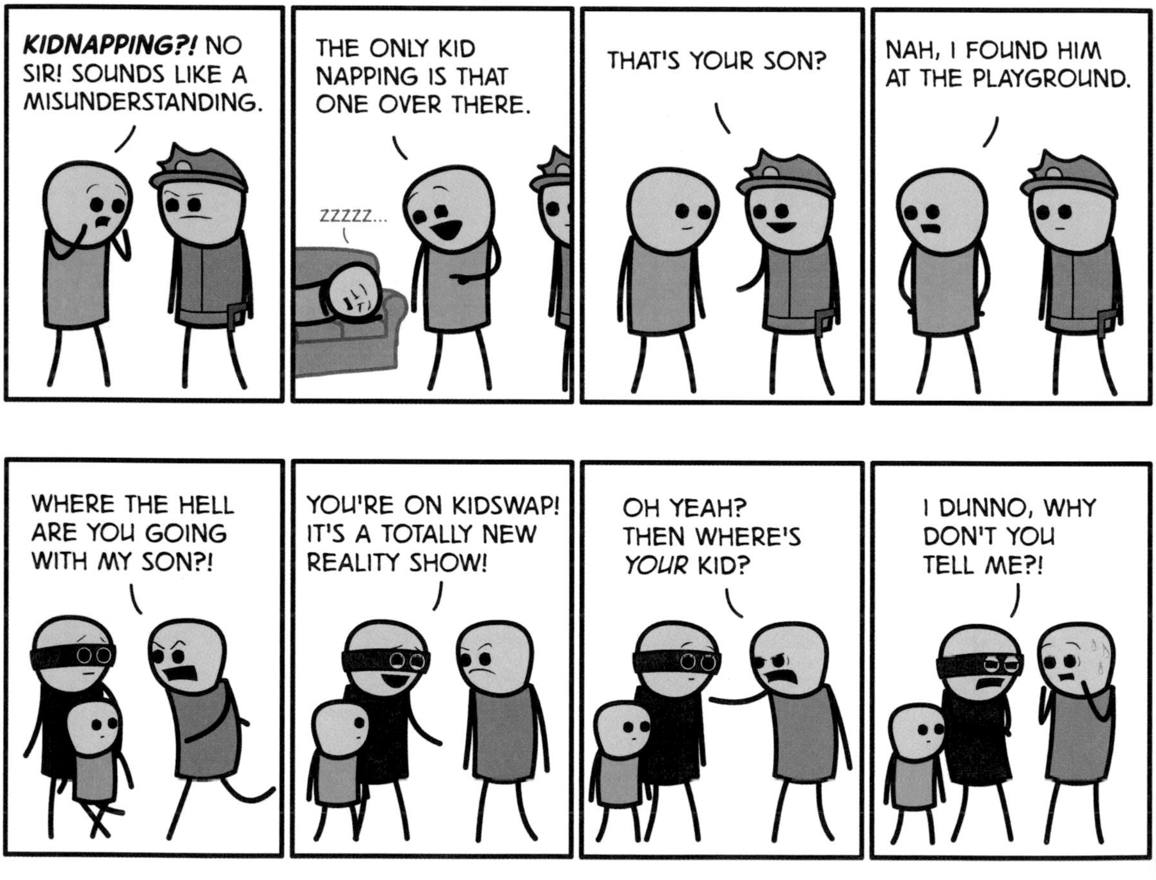

KIDNAPPING?! NO SIR! SOUNDS LIKE A MISUNDERSTANDING.
THE ONLY KID NAPPING IS THAT ONE OVER THERE.
ZZZZZ...
THAT'S YOUR SON?
NAH, I FOUND HIM AT THE PLAYGROUND.
WHERE THE HELL ARE YOU GOING WITH MY SON?!
YOU'RE ON KIDSWAP! IT'S A TOTALLY NEW REALITY SHOW!
OH YEAH? THEN WHERE'S YOUR KID?
I DUNNO, WHY DON'T YOU TELL ME?!

Your Only Chance

You've read the previous chapter of this book with the expression of a man who's just been forced to lick a popsicle made from bulldog spit. "No icky stuff for me," says the grown adult that is you. "I'm not gonna put my junk in there, it'll get all gooey! I still want a baby, though." Your words are definitely the words of a sane, mature human being who is absolutely up to the task of rearing a child, and they resound in my ears like a whisper in a tin can. Whilst I cannot wholeheartedly recommend this risky loophole, consider it the up, up, down, down, left, right, left, right, B, A of babymaking.

Just kidnap some kid instead.

Kidnapping is the à la carte of child-rearing. You have the opportunity to choose from a range of heights, ages, hair colors, and personalities from the very get-go, kinda like a create-a-character mode with really good graphics. Consider whether their current father is nearby. Is he? Does he look miserable? Perhaps he'd only be happy to have you nab the spoils of his loins. Observe carefully.

Upon choosing your child, maybe in a park from a bush or on a bus, smartly and confidently approach them and ask straight-up (don't be a creep), "Can I be your new dad?" If the child gives you a resounding "YES! I am an apple that wants to fall farther from my tree, take me," give pause before proceeding. You might be talking to an apple. If you have made sure that you are not in fact talking to an apple, after much deliberation, invite the child to come along with you. Congratulations, you have become a father without the inconvenience of your spouse being pregnant.

The authorities will confirm your new fatherhood officially by phone, sending you what is known as an "Amber Alert" to congratulate you on your passion for fatherhood. Now go, go explore your newfound parentage. Don't stop going. Go as far away as you can. Now you're ready to read the rest of this book. Better read it quick.

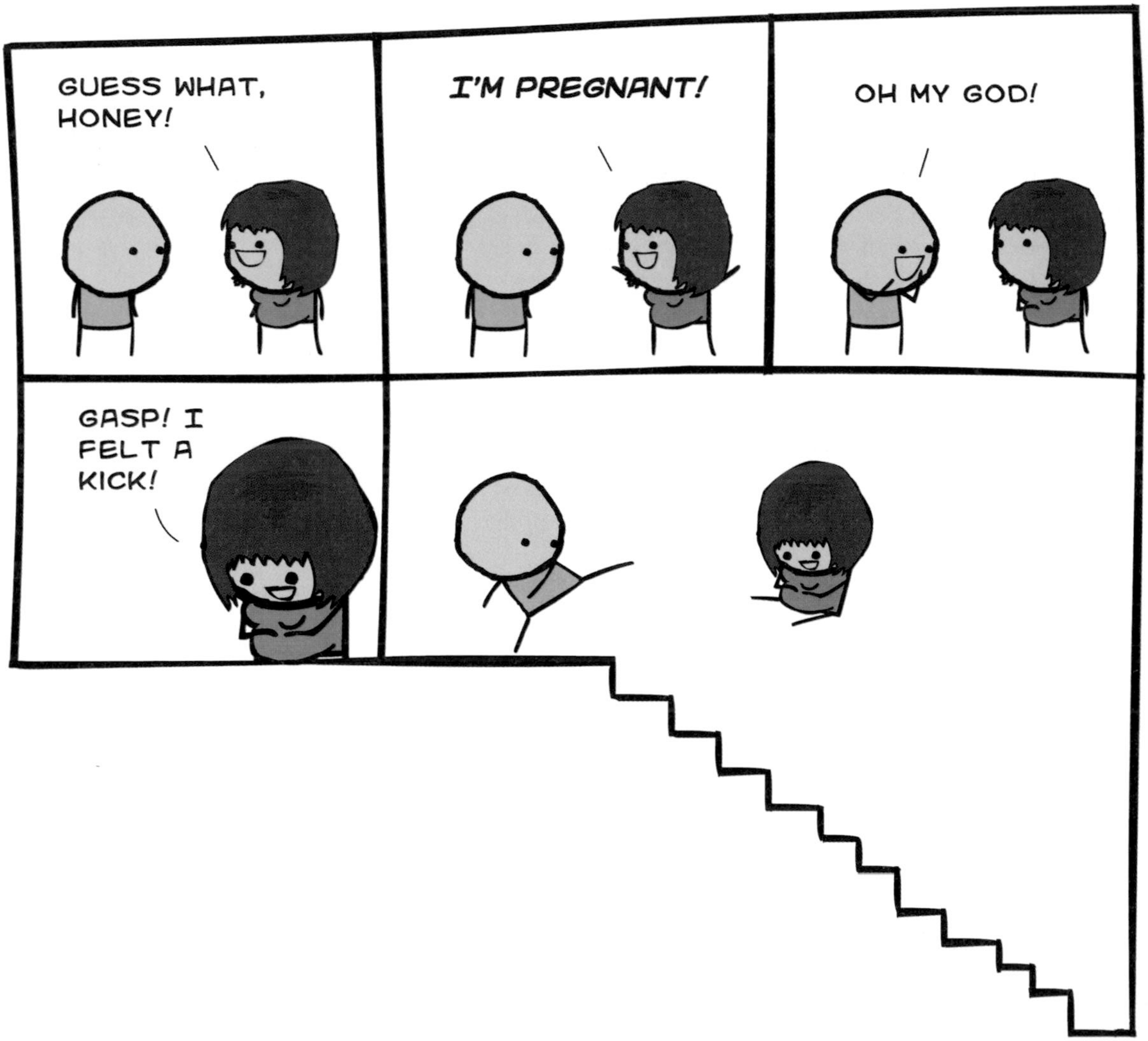
GUESS WHAT, HONEY!
I'M PREGNANT!
OH MY GOD!
GASP! I FELT A KICK!

Pregnancy

If your spouse feels kicks and punches during pregnancy, that can only mean one thing – your child is already a violent offender at best and a wife-beating misogynist at worst. That kid's attacking your spouse! Defend her honor. Fight back. Land a swift jab or two to the womb. Show that prospective mothertrucker who's boss. Spar with it. Roundhouse kick that sucker so it knows who the big daddy is. Your spouse will greatly appreciate your valiance, and your child will eventually enter into the world with an immediate understanding of your absolute, crushing authority. Your significant other will absolutely not kick your ass, baby in stomach, like some Krang meat mech for so much as laying a finger on her.

Be prepared to fist fight during the childbirth process. Maintain a strong fighting stance as you stand at the bedside, as the battle may not be over yet. If your child comes out crying, that means you've won. Yeah, you lost, kid. Suck it down. Weep hard those salty tears of defeat. Down them like the cocktail of conquest they are. When the doctor presents to you the spoils of your groins, hold it by the back of the head and stare into its eyes. Do not flinch. Whisper through gritted teeth, "Who's the boss, bitch?" If you feel fear, do not show it. Do not show weakness. No, stop shaking. Stop it. Good lord, you are pathetic. You're off to a terrible start.

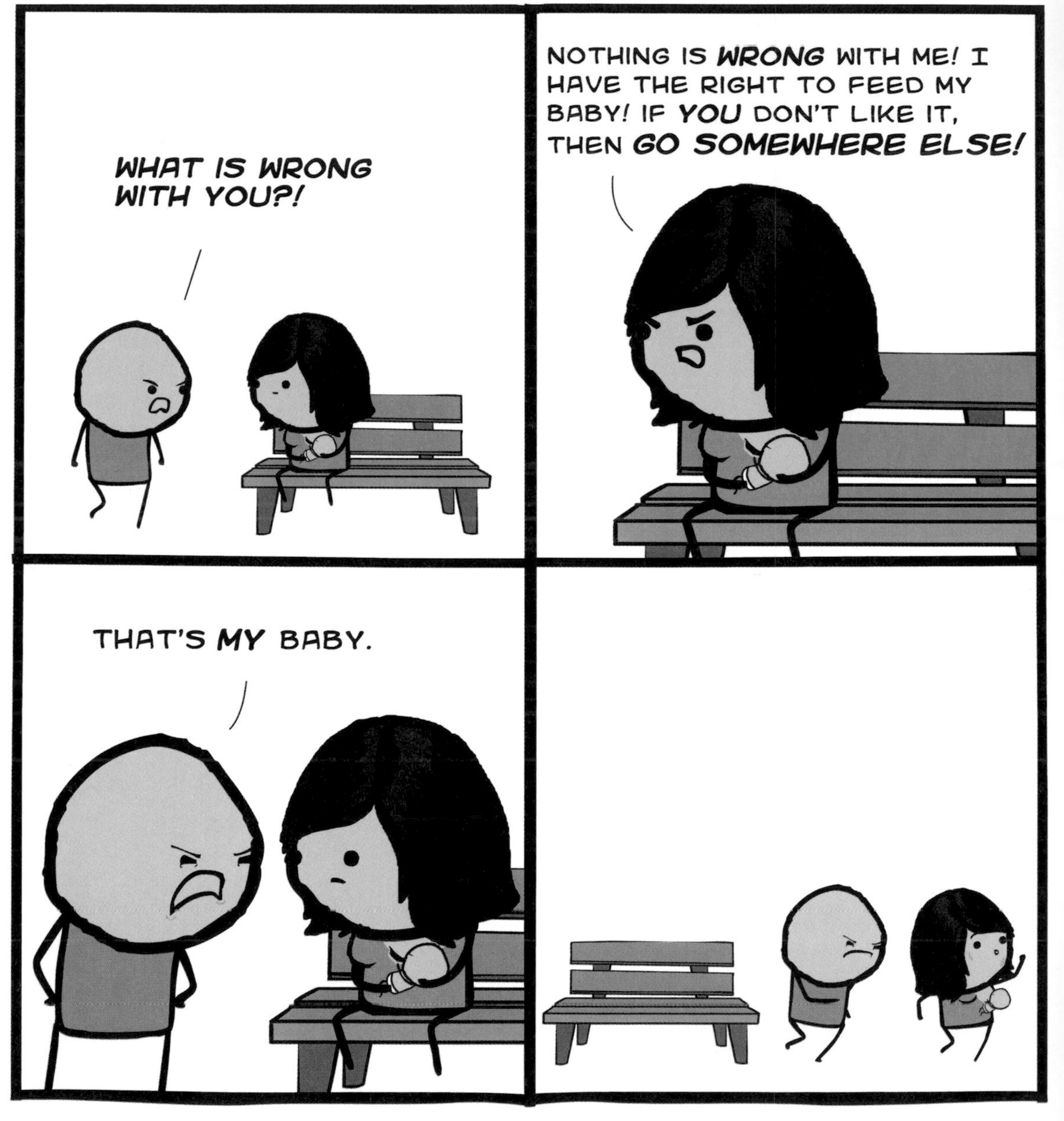

WHAT IS WRONG WITH YOU?!
NOTHING IS WRONG WITH ME! I HAVE THE RIGHT TO FEED MY BABY! IF YOU DON'T LIKE IT, THEN GO SOMEWHERE ELSE!
THAT'S MY BABY.

Breastfeeding

A taboo subject for some, being fed with tits can conjure feelings of discomfort, revulsion, and even faint arousal in the minds of some members of the public. If you are one of these people, then I put this forth to you—why the attitude? Search deep within yourself. Deeper. Not in there, that's gross. Keep going. Feel something? Pull it out. Ah, there it is: jealousy.

Look down at your useless milk duds. There they are, poking out of the landscape of your chest, like old war bunkers erected in case of emergency but never put to use. They lie beyond dormant and dilapidated, like a Chevy without an engine. I can see your scorn as you look down upon them, like sad scars from a buxom life you never had. Try tweaking them. Tweak them like you're trying to find some acid jazz radio station from Jupiter. Nope. Nothing.

"Why can't I weep delicious dairy treats from my nipples?!" I hear you weep in your own mind. Go on, desperately reach down and try to suckle them with your own lips, right now, as you read this book. Try to touch them with your tongue. Reach as hard as you can. Use your hands to pull them up. Now, look in the mirror at your desperate visage trying to suckle your own teats. That's right, you do look pathetic. Your tits are impotent and extinct. Sob. Sob hard. Oh yeah. I like that. Keep doing it.

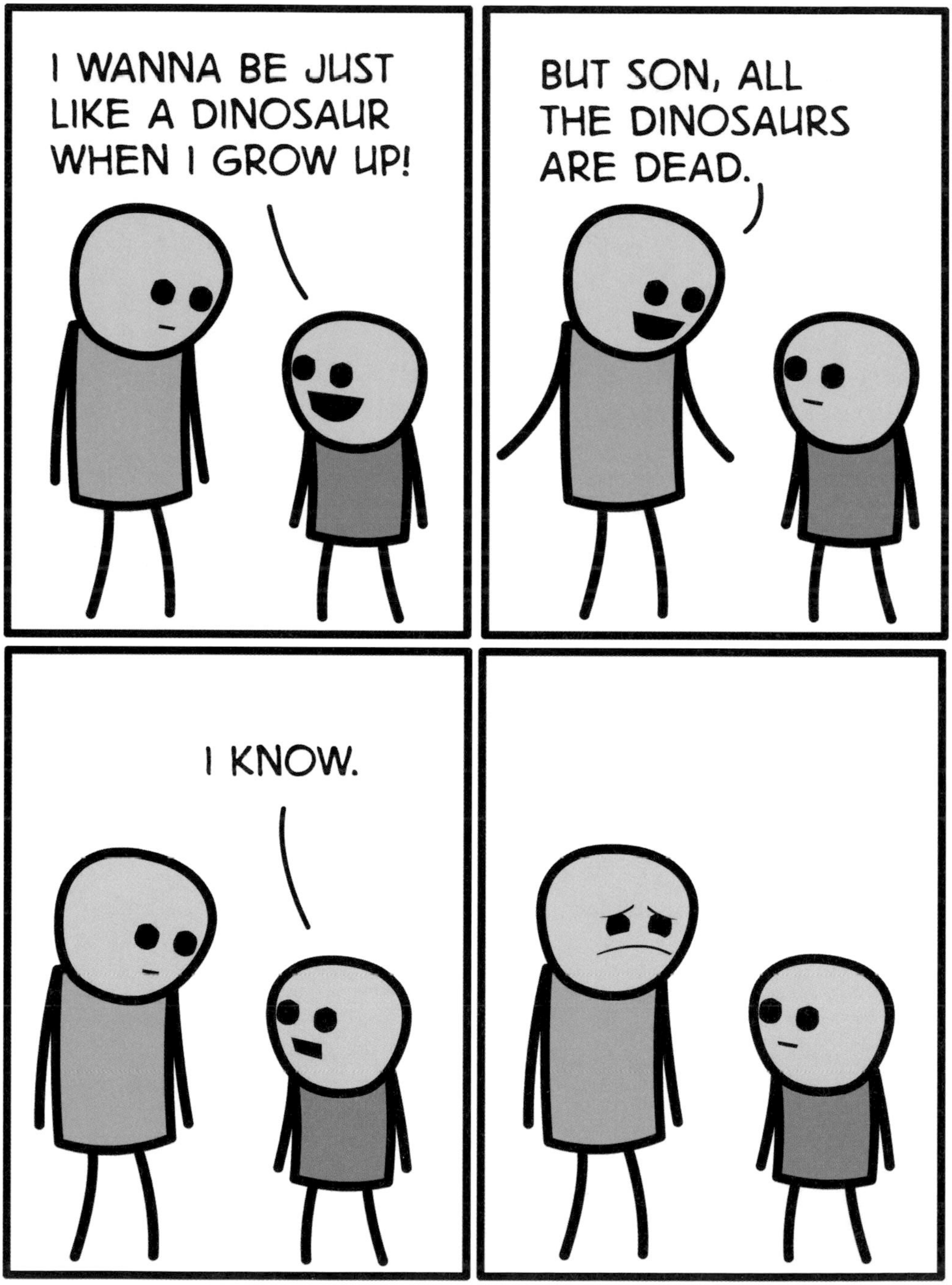
I WANNA BE JUST LIKE A DINOSAUR WHEN I GROW UP!
BUT SON, ALL THE DINOSAURS ARE DEAD.
I KNOW.

Lofty Aspirations

Children have lofty aspirations. When I was a youth, my father told me that I could be anything if I put my mind to it, as long as it was far away from him. Like most children, I reached for the sky with an interminable desire to drive a truck, or a lawnmower. Or a boat. Any of those would have been fine in my book. Which this is.

Some of my associates dreamed even more gargantuanly than I. I have one childhood friend named Lester, who once told me that he wanted to be a Brontosaurus when he grew up. This was in the late 90s/early 2000s, when we were told we could be anything we wanted to be, as long as we worked hard. Sure enough, I observed Lester apply himself all throughout school to study being a Brontosaurus, where he eventually graduated as valedictorian before being accepted into an honors program at an Ivy League Brontosaurus college outside Boston. Seven grueling years later, just as he had finally earned a PhD in being a Brontosaurus, the Great Recession hit and all of the jobs in his field disappeared. Today, he solemnly flips burgers at a local Braums, which is complicated by the fact that he Is now a 70 Ft. long dinosaur. I last heard that he had applied for disability benefits but was found to be still fit for work. Now his baby boomer parents ridicule him for "being entitled" and "expecting a free lunch." Pfft, millennials, eh?

Consider this tale a cautionary one. Don't let your kid be the Brontosaurus. As for me, I've achieved my dream of driving a truck and drinking every day, which is a fantastic stroke of luck, as no one would employ me for anything else.

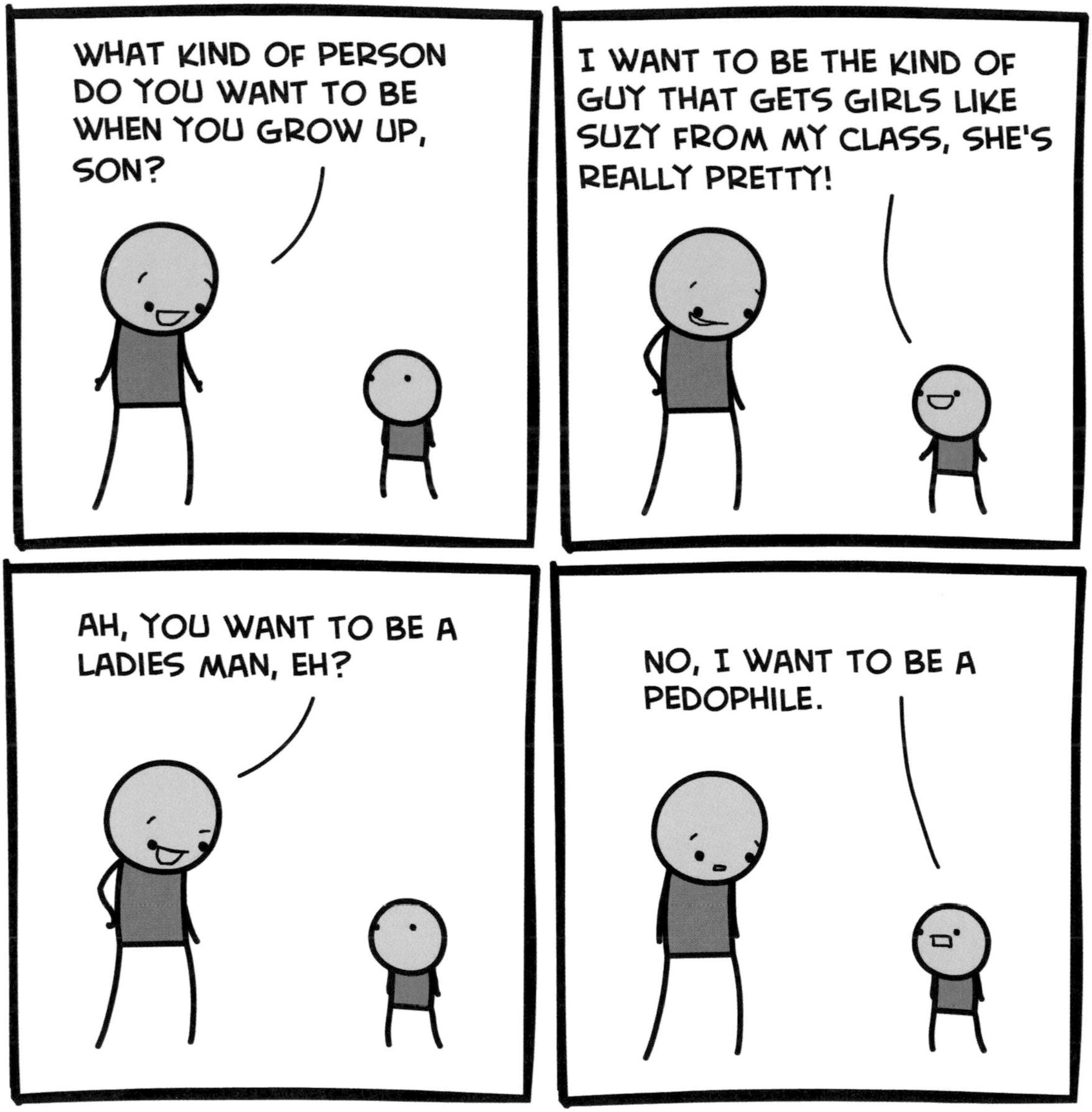
WHAT KIND OF PERSON DO YOU WANT TO BE WHEN YOU GROW UP, SON?
I WANT TO BE THE KIND OF GUY THAT GETS GIRLS LIKE SUZY FROM MY CLASS, SHE'S REALLY PRETTY!
AH, YOU WANT TO BE A LADIES MAN, EH?
NO, I WANT TO BE A PEDOPHILE.

Nope

Not a great aspiration.

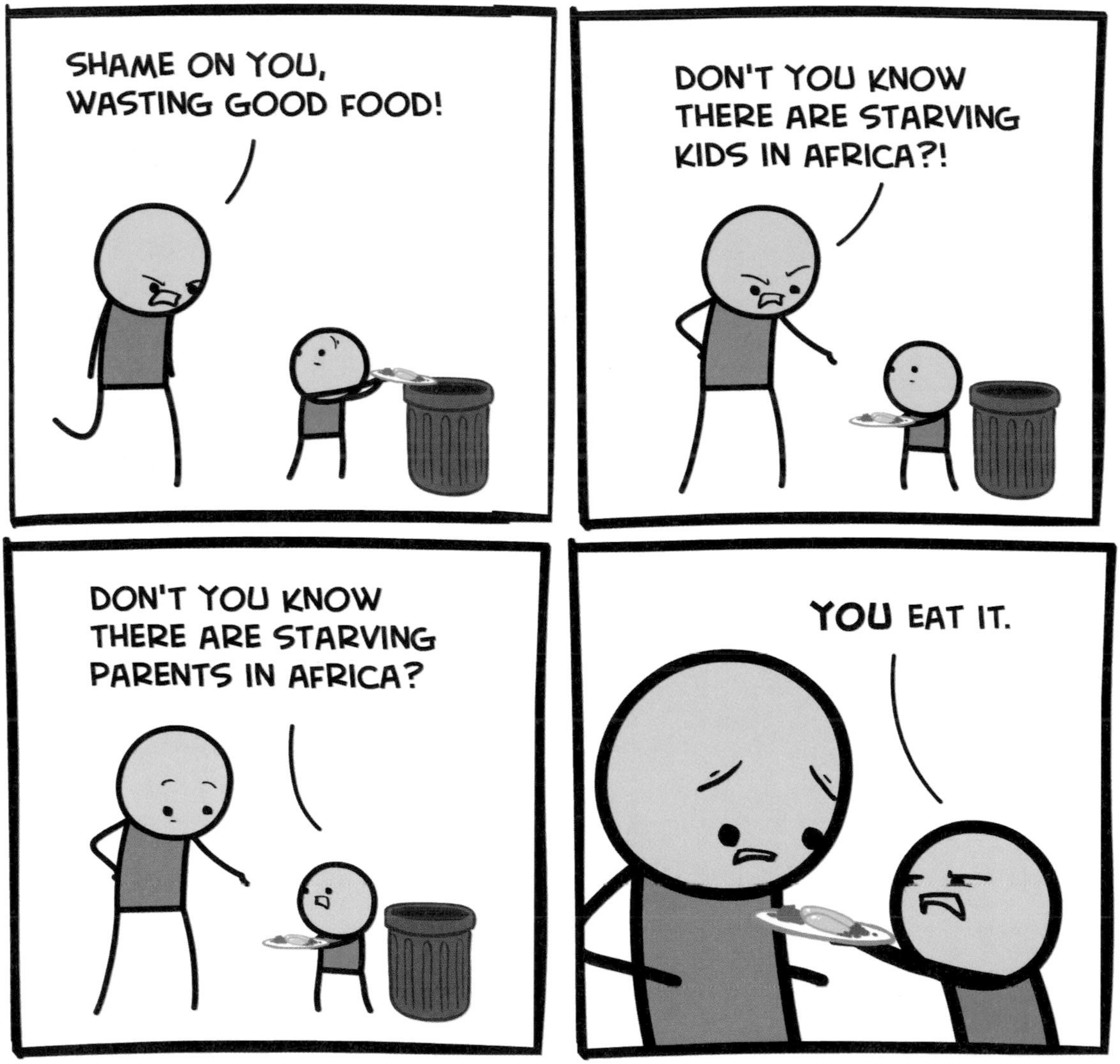
SHAME ON YOU, WASTING GOOD FOOD!
DON'T YOU KNOW THERE ARE STARVING KIDS IN AFRICA?!
DON'T YOU KNOW THERE ARE STARVING PARENTS IN AFRICA?
YOU EAT IT.

Those Starving Kids in Africa

You talk about those starving kids in Africa so much, so put your food where their mouth is. Go to Africa. Cook for them instead of your ungrateful spoiled sprog. Go and spoil those little African children rotten. Feed them until they pop. If they complain about being full, tell them, "Don't you know there's one starving kid in America?" Now you're not only an A+ parent but a B- humanitarian. Good job, you.

Cramming food down your kid's throat to the point of regurgitation is a valuable lesson that applies itself like a bumper sticker to the wheezing jalopy that is the automobile of life as a whole. At quick glance, life's possibilities present themselves like a succulent steak dinner. The meat your personal affairs, the potatoes your prospects, and the garnish your daily obligations. Once you dig deeper, however, you find the meat to be gray and lacking tenderness, the potatoes to be devoid of any real meaning, and the garnish to be an unwanted, aggravating sprinkle that is to be removed from your ever-shrinking plate before you can even try to find a modicum of enjoyment in what's salvageable. So chow down, kid. There's plenty more.

UGH, I HATE HOMEWORK! I DON'T WANNA FINISH IT!
SHAME ON YOU, NOT FINISHING YOUR HOMEWORK!
DON'T YOU KNOW THERE ARE STUPID KIDS IN AFRICA?

I DON'T WANNA EAT THIS. THIS SHIT'S GROSS.
SON. THERE ARE CHILDREN STARVING IN AFRICA.
NOW FINISH YOUR FOOD SO THEY CAN'T GET ANY OF IT.

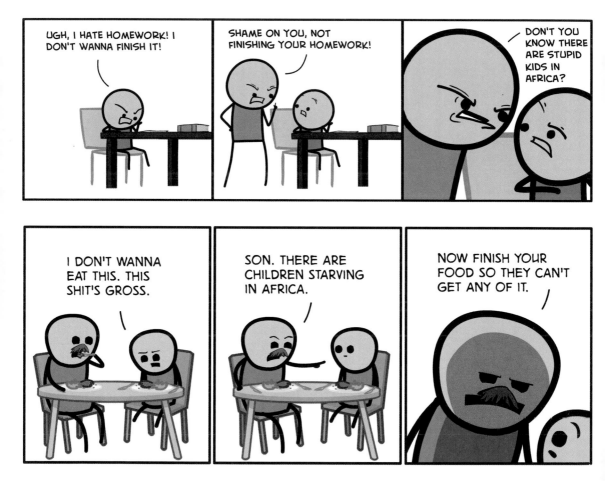

Those Stupid Kids in Africa

You've imparted the wisdom of telling your nipper about hungry children in Africa, but do they know that there are stupid children there as well? You're really down on Africa, aren't you? What is your issue?

Take a similar approach to homework as you do with food. Cram it down your kid's throat. Literally. Make them chow down on the damn homework. Every last scrap of paper. Make a corny dad joke about digesting information. If they call you in to school and ask you why your child never brings in homework, you can make the excuse that they ate it—and you wouldn't be fibbing.

Speaking of that timeless trope, why do children always blame the dog for eating homework, anyway? Are they aware of some deep conspiracy that we're not privy to? Are dogs intentionally trying to digest our children's homework? Are they perhaps attempting to absorb human knowledge in order to use it against us, and some day carry out a callous canine coup to impart themselves as the true masters within our ancient, interspecific dynamic? Don't ask me. This is just a book about parenting. If you came to this book with that query on your lips in hopes of an answer, you've made a grave error. Go and return this book immediately.

Those Starving Kids in Africa (Again)

Seriously dude, what is your beef with Africa? Lay off. I have nothing else to say about this. Leave me alone.

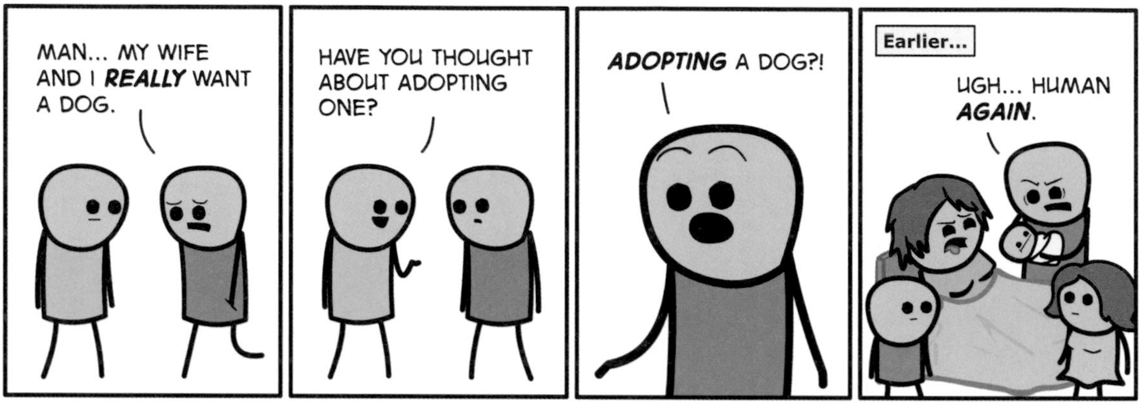

MAN... MY WIFE AND I ***REALLY*** WANT A DOG.
HAVE YOU THOUGHT ABOUT ADOPTING ONE?
ADOPTING A DOG?!
Earlier...
UGH... HUMAN ***AGAIN***.

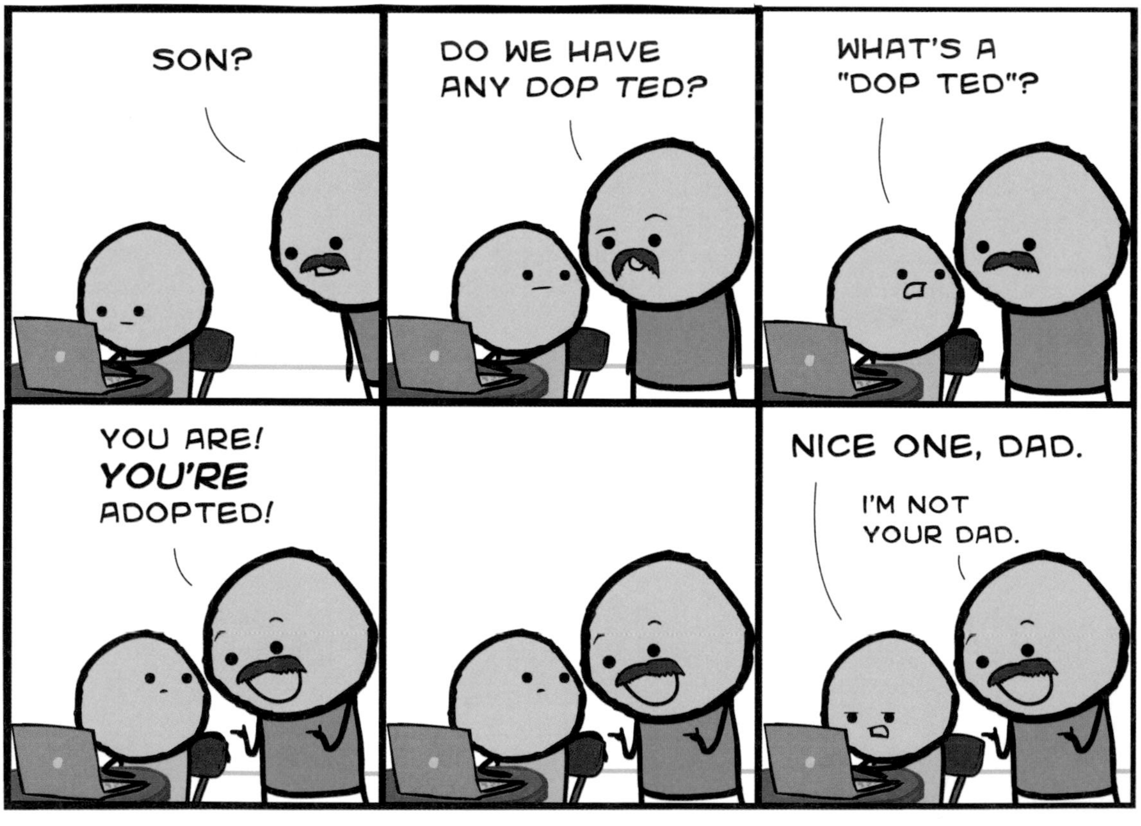

SON?
DO WE HAVE ANY DOP TED?
WHAT'S A "DOP TED"?
YOU ARE! ***YOU'RE*** ADOPTED!
NICE ONE, DAD.
I'M NOT YOUR DAD.

Dealing With Adoption

It's happened. Some big cuckoo's gone and laid a cloak-and-dagger cackleberry in your once tidy nest, and now you're left caring with the result. You didn't even get to use your dick. What the hell is this? Only this time, you've let this happen willingly. Go you. You've lovingly brought a human being into your home, much like you would a spaniel or a microwave. Life is good. You keep them free from their origins for now. They are embryonic, enthused, and hungry to observe the delicately arranged, pastel-colored world you have built for them. You don't need to drop any bombs on it like some sort of Duplo Dresden. They may not quite share your palette, but their features are still vague and forthcoming. There's no question that this is your child for now. You are one proud parent.

As your child slowly sprouts towards adolescence, however, it starts to become increasingly clear to them that something's not right. "Why don't I have your freakish hooked nose?" your misappropriated minor bleats. "Why don't I have the same squinty, black-eyed-pea eyes as you, Papa?" "Why is my jaw chiseled and virile, whilst yours looks like a beach ball in a hammock? Why Papa, why?" First of all, holy crap, when did your child become so handsome? It's now painfully obvious that they have been carved from DNA of steel, rather than the drunkenly typed gobbledygook that resembles your lamentable genetic information. Your child chips at you increasingly day-by-day until you finally snap. You fucking lose it. "BECAUSE I'M NOT YOUR FUCKING DAD, OKAY?! FUCKING HAPPY NOW??!"

Oop, now you've done it. You shouldn't have done that. That's not the right way to deal with that at all.

SOMEDAY SON, THIS WILL ALL BE YOURS!
CRIPPLING DEBT
DEBT DEBT ALL SORTS OF DEBT YOU ARE TRULY FUCKED IN THE
UTT. I'M SO SORRY. BLAH DE BLAH DE BLAH DE BLAH DE BLAH
O FUCK YOURSELF -38438434834038043
ERIOUSLY GO FUCK YOURSELF - 3943843
3493478390439473947394374937439473 7
39047394739473947397439743743
904930473470937437490274290472 4
072904
24-28-04280428-04-0824-02840-
284-2-8428-48-0248-28-0428-0428-48-28-
2-482-8428-48-284-28-428-48-248-28-4-
THE LIGHT OF THE SHINING SUN WILL ALWAYS GIVE WAY TO
ABSOLUTE DARKNESS AT SOME POINT IN THE DAY- DO NOT
HESITATE TO TAKE HERES ANOTHER BIG PILE OF SHIT THAT I
HAVE TO TYPE DOWN JUST TO MAKE IT CLEAR ALSO HERES SOME
RED TEXT RED3 4930438473493043439749394343743743473470394
The coyote (US /ka?'o?ti, 'ka?o?t/;[a] Canis latrans) is a
canine native to North America. It is smaller than its
close relative, the gray wolf, being roughly the North
American equivalent to the Old World golden jackal, though

Inheritance

Debt—financial, social, or sexual—is the undesirable yet inescapable monkey that swings unrepentantly from the backbone of life. The saving grace in this metaphorical case of dorsal scoliosis is the relief that you can always attempt to defer, at least financially. So why not, in this instance, hold off paying your debts until you are dead? Said monkey will indiscriminately leap from your resourceless rachis and pounce onto your next of kin like the callous catarrhine it is, and your sprog will learn a valuable lesson for them to pass on to their future offspring. Explain your intentions to your child no later than the age of 3, so that they can gain a thorough understanding early on. If they fail to understand or forget, that's on them.

If they express any concern, you can soften the blow by reminding them that there's only a 50/50 chance that they'll inherit your slowly-petrifying rheumatism, your innate and unquenchable desire to drink alone, and your toes turning a peculiar shade of yellow at the age of 40. On the plus side, once you desperately complete the mortal coil marathon that is your miserable existence and escape to the applauding ether for all eternity, your child will be able to fully indulge in your peculiar collection of Pogs and Cheetos shaped like wild animals. They'll soon learn that they can't eat Pogs, and that the Cheetos have long since evaporated. Such is life.

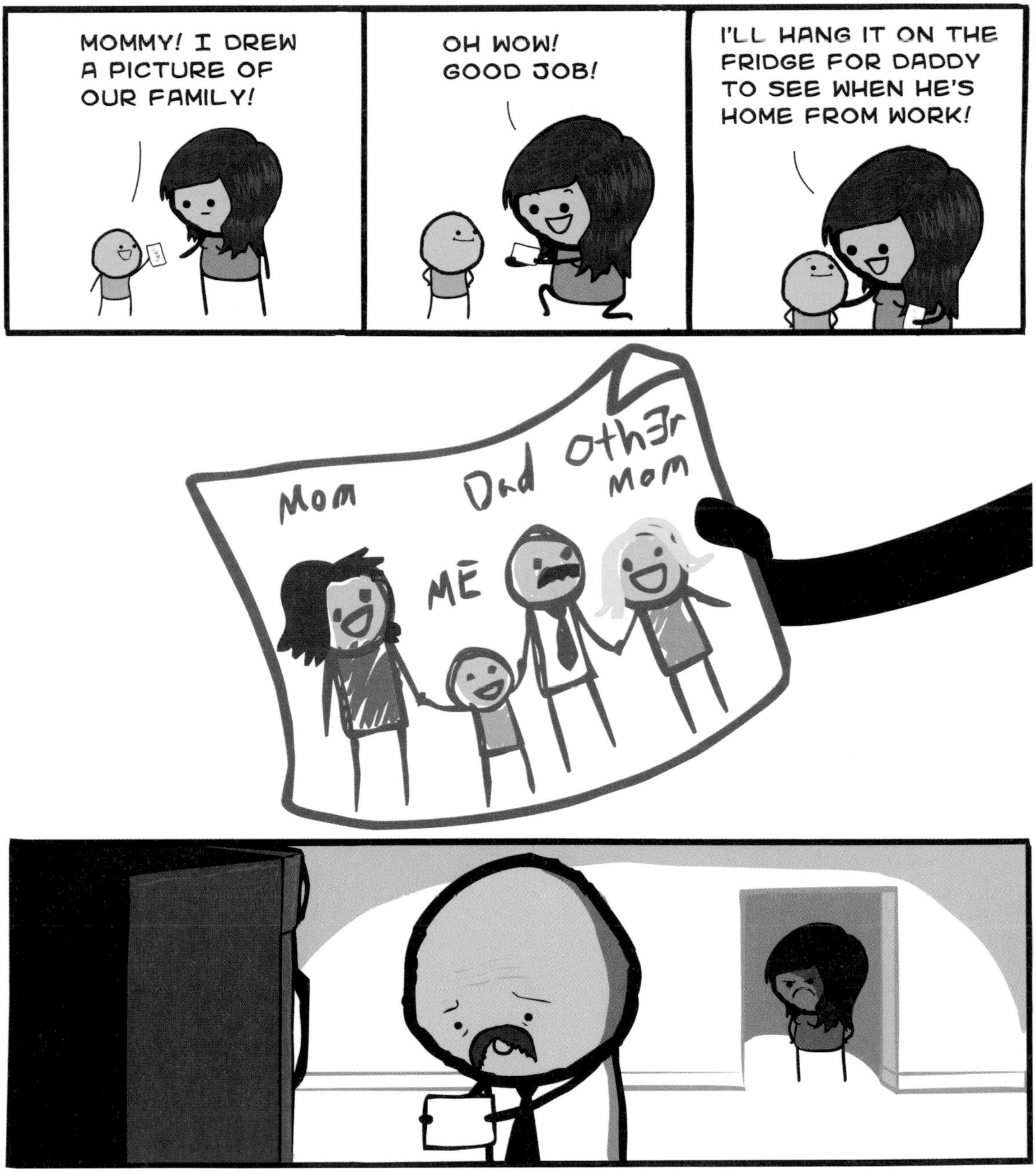
MOMMY! I DREW A PICTURE OF OUR FAMILY!
OH WOW! GOOD JOB!
I'LL HANG IT ON THE FRIDGE FOR DADDY TO SEE WHEN HE'S HOME FROM WORK!
Mom
Dad
OthƎr Mom
ME

Other Mom

So. You've been playing away from home because you really like Twister, but there's only Checkers in the house. Now your voyeuristic little prick of a child has, through their own sweet, innocent naiveté, felt the need to commit their findings to posterity in the form of a drawing of your squalid little double life. Now you have to explain to Checkers.

Consider this a golden opportunity. Deny everything at first, but then gently encourage conversation towards the fact that your child draws some pretty erotic stuff. Look at the round, voluptuous sweatercows on Other Mom! Are those sheer stockings and high heels he drew on her? Man, he really gave her a pair of lips that can polish—and that thong she's wearing makes her look like she's trying to cut some Parmesan from the interior of her posterior. Don't dwell on that thought too heavily.

Why would little infant Timmy draw something only fit for the farthest reaches of the top shelf in some webby, nicotine-stained corner store? Is he trying to tell us something? Maybe this is his desire? Maybe the one wish our innocuous infant holds deep within his heart is for daddy to have a "slammin' bit of secondary snatch" around the house? That sounds like a term your child would definitely use, if only he were older and more eloquent. Carefully articulate this to your spouse using this exact wording. She wouldn't deny a boy his childhood dream, would she?

Oh, she would. She'd crush his dreams in a flea's minute. Let her know that she's a heartless monster.

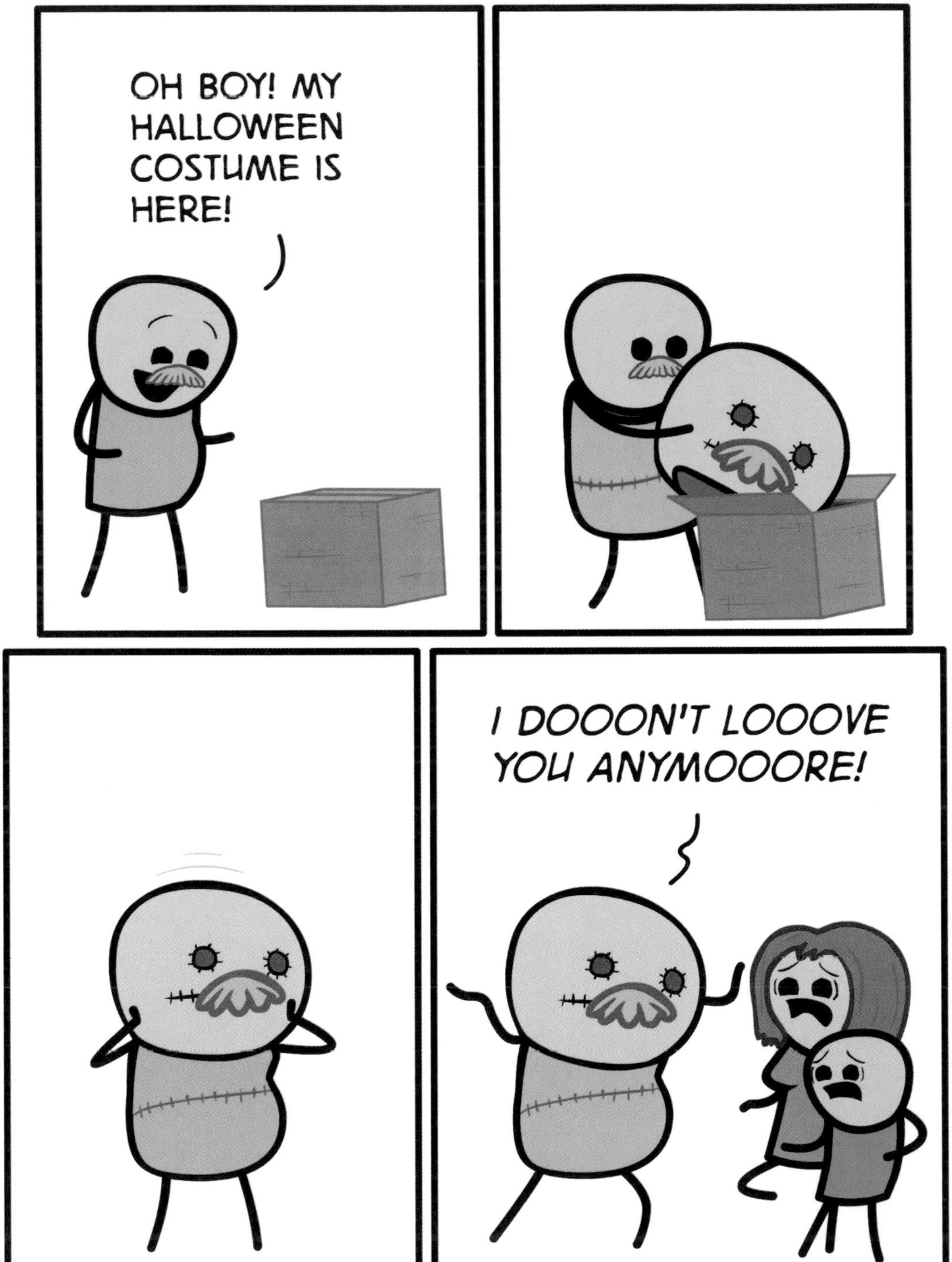
OH BOY! MY HALLOWEEN COSTUME IS HERE!
I DOOON'T LOOOVE YOU ANYMOOORE!

Sorry Baby, But This Cat Can't Be Tied Down . . . It's Time for Me to Make Another Town Happy

It's gone. The love you had for your family no longer flows, but barely beads onto your dry tongue as you desperately lick around the ring pull on the can, searching for anything that'll stop you from kicking down the front door and taking the midnight train going anywhere. Alas, it's all bereft. You're out of options, and it's time to inform the family that you have no choice but to kick them to the curb.

Telling your child that you don't love them anymore is like telling your cab driver to get out of the vehicle. Here you are, both intimately bound to the same familiar, preset pilgrimage, your companion suckling and preying on your ever-increasing fare like a gummy mantis, when suddenly you swipe the only thing truly binding you both from under their feet. You've mashed their potatoes, and all they know is potatoes. It's time to explain mashed potatoes.

Therapists often suggest puppets to act out feelings, but what to do when you must act out a lack of feelings? Try full-blown custom costumes, as in the example accompanying. Order costumes that resemble each of you. Sit your family down when they arrive. Have your child wear a full-size costume of you, complete with a cold dinner and a warm bottle of beer for full effect. Don the costume of your child and perform coldly honest impressions of them, using clever phrases like, "Durr hurr look at me," and, "I'm a smelly pee pee, please dislike me." Have your spouse wear the costume of herself, so she can get a feel for what it's like to be able to be herself again once you've gone.

Is your child inside your brain yet? Do they understand? If so, they should already be out the door, still wearing that same costume of you, speeding as fast as they can to fulfill the life that you've always wanted via identity theft. Now they get it.

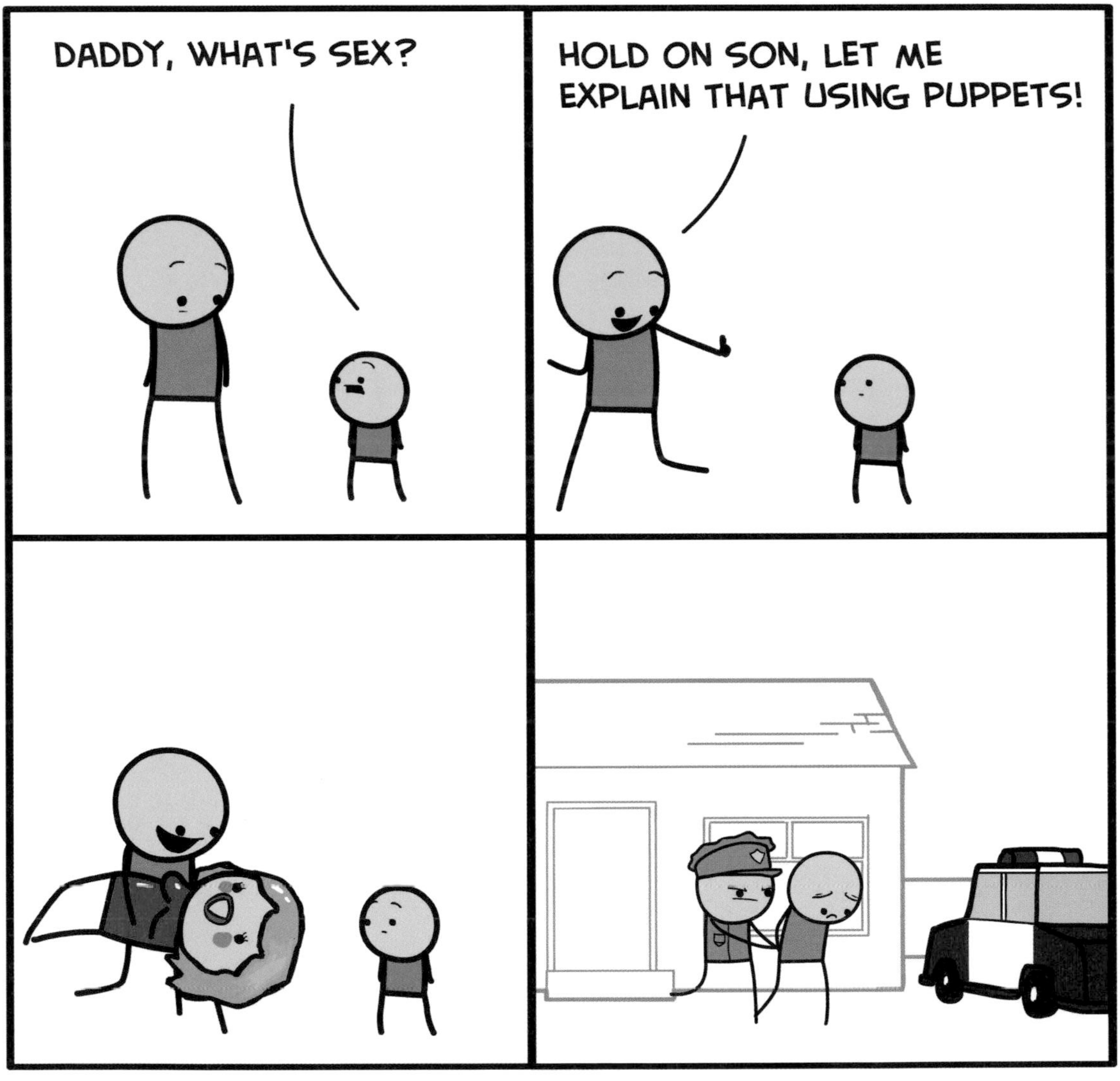
DADDY, WHAT'S SEX?
HOLD ON SON, LET ME EXPLAIN THAT USING PUPPETS!

Hard Talk

Definitely use puppets here. Do not make your family wear costumes.

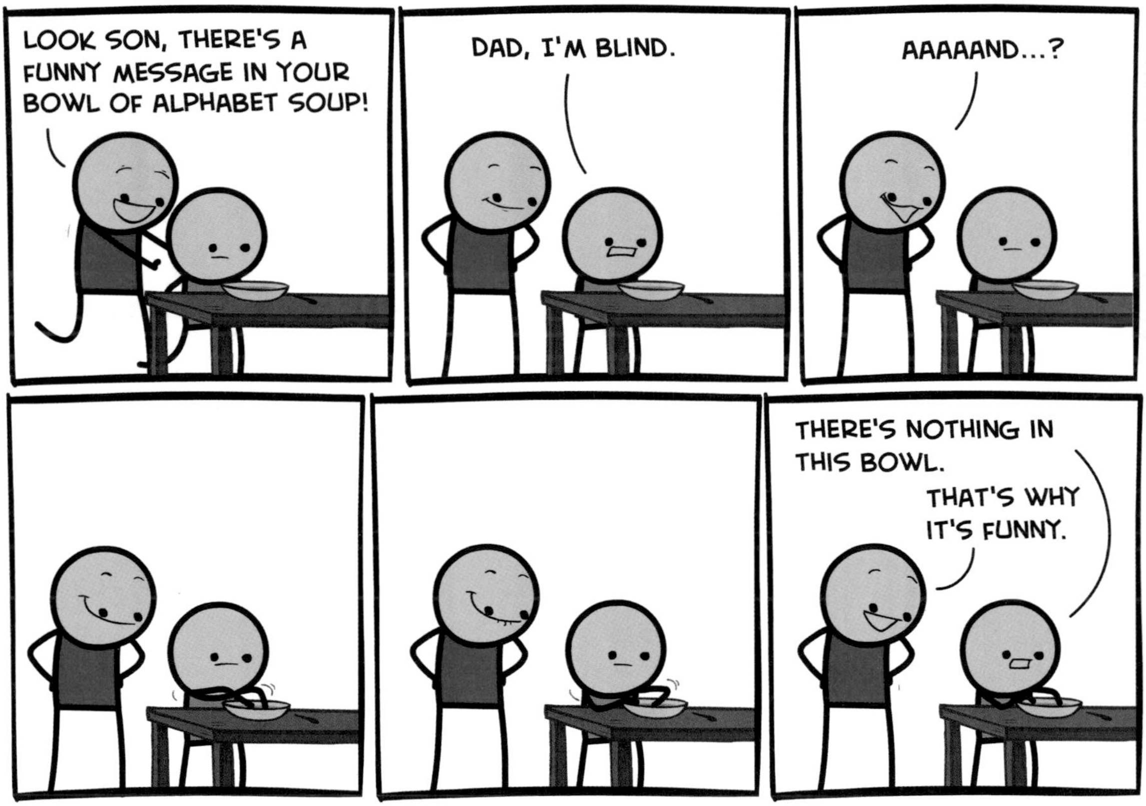
LOOK SON, THERE'S A FUNNY MESSAGE IN YOUR BOWL OF ALPHABET SOUP!
DAD, I'M BLIND.
AAAAAND...?
THERE'S NOTHING IN THIS BOWL.
THAT'S WHY IT'S FUNNY.

Ha Ha, Look at No Eyes Over Here

If your offspring has a bad case of the blinds, like one particularly infamous bat, or a bookcase, fret not. You may feel like you've been spurned with faulty goods like the bitter old bastard you are, but I'm afraid you can't return it from whence it came (or whence you ca . . . ? No? Never mind. We're all grown-ups here). You may feel like you've been blessed with the last old banger in the dealership, but that doesn't mean you can't take it out for a spin. Go on, get your jollies. Prank the bejeezus out of them with all sorts of sight-starved swindles and scrapes. It's not your fault. You didn't ask for this. If eyes came as part of a customization option, you'd have spent the extra ten bucks. Your child forgot the eyes before he came out, like you do with your keys or a cellphone. Now it must deal with the consequences.

Leave any sense of remorse on compassion's doorstep as you set up all sorts of fun traps and scrapes for your ocular-omitted oik like some sort of weird, bizarro Home Alone climax. Hold this nugget in the back of your mind – pranking blind kids is fine because they can't use their eyes, meaning they're unable to get sad and cry. Also, please don't tell them anything that I've said in this book. I'm legitimately scared of the wrath of your blind children. I don't need to feel blind eyes not staring daggers at me in the street. Promise this book right now. I don't care if you're in front of anyone. Do it.

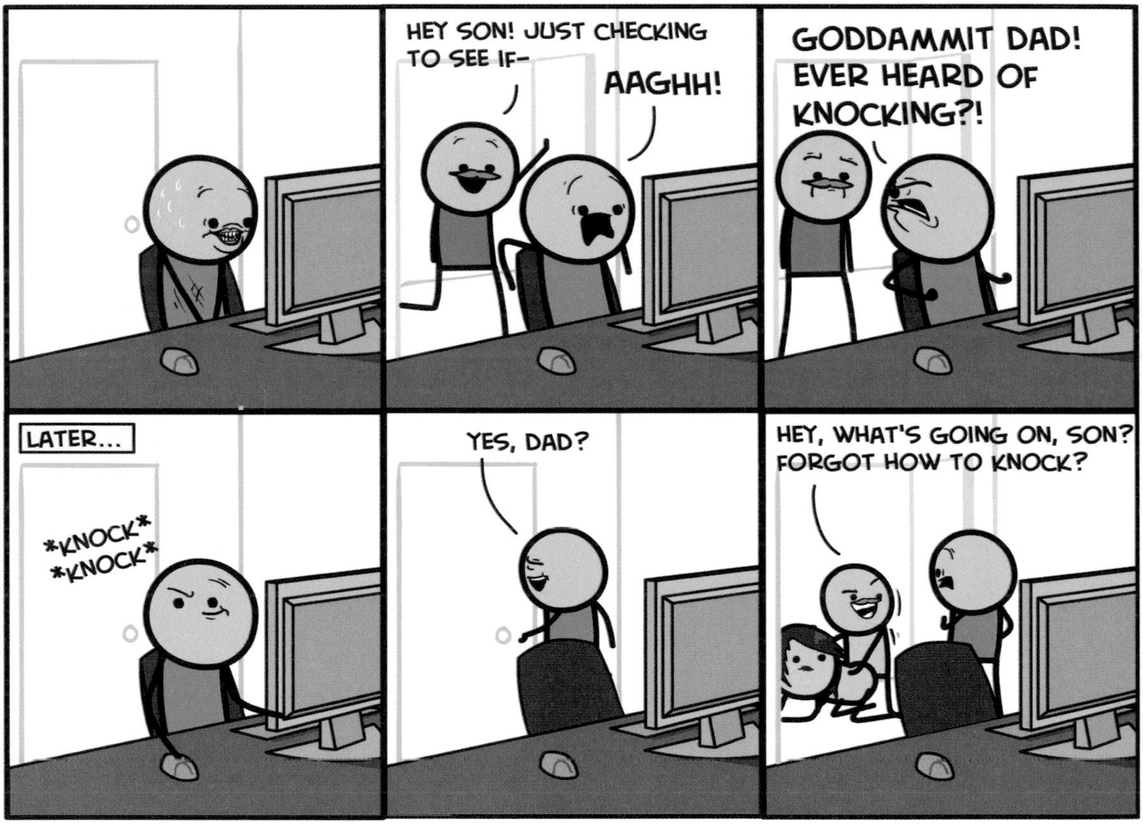
HEY SON! JUST CHECKING TO SEE IF-
AAGHH!
GODDAMMIT DAD! EVER HEARD OF KNOCKING?!
LATER...
KNOCK *KNOCK*
YES, DAD?
HEY, WHAT'S GOING ON, SON? FORGOT HOW TO KNOCK?

Your New Mission

You and your little boy have successfully navigated the coarse rapids of juvenile life, and now here you are. You're a little saggier, your legs get pins and needles easier, and to be honest, you might have Type-2 diabetes. Without looking at your thorough medical history, I can't say for sure, but you should maybe set up an appointment.

However, mocking your trivial changes, your child has undergone a complete transformation from rosy-arsed cherub to teenage ogre—and he's very confused. What was once merely an unremarkable skintag used for expelling urine, is now being given all the poorly-hidden attention that your son has to offer. Now he wants to urinate in an entirely different way. He wants to urinate into a woman. As far as his understanding goes, anyway. Or into a man. Or nearly anything, really. Whichever. I'm not here to judge your child's preferences. It's the year you're reading this book in. There's no place for that.

Your child, in a sustained effort to educate himself on his newfound interest, will endeavor to seek a full audio/visual tutorial on the internet, privately. Once this process begins, you will automatically receive a package in the mail from Parent HQ. You have new orders, should you choose to accept them. Your role is now one of espionage. You must catch them red-handed in the act at any cost.

Such begins a years-long game of cat and mouse. Learn every creak in the stairs. Be attuned to minute volume changes in music blaring from your child's bedroom. Minimize the volume of your own footsteps as much as you can. When you've finally caught them with their guard completely lowered, barge into their room with feigned horror and surprise. Act as if they have just murdered and smelted a 30-strong collection of golden crickets that you excavated in Giza, raining ten hundred gallons of shame upon them for the audacity of exploring their own bodies. Dust your hands off satisfied afterwards, because you just brought your 10/10 parenting game.

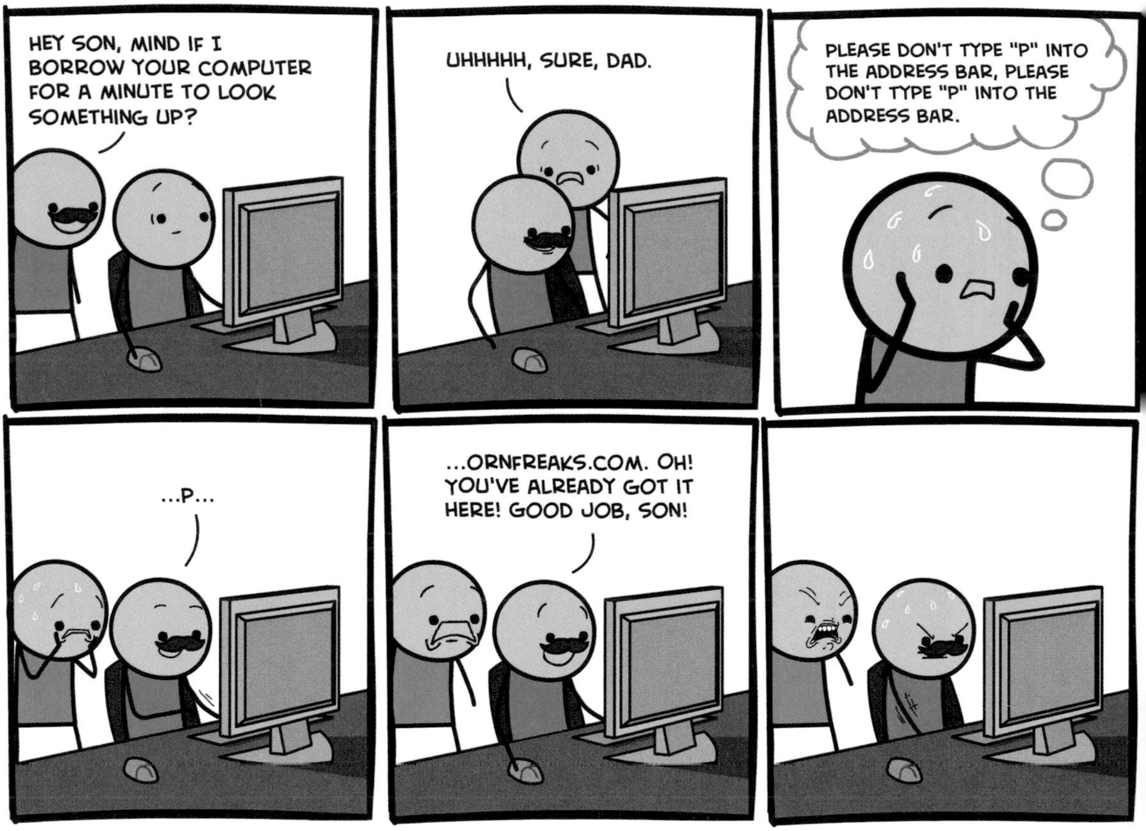
HEY SON, MIND IF I BORROW YOUR COMPUTER FOR A MINUTE TO LOOK SOMETHING UP?
UHHHHH, SURE, DAD.
PLEASE DON'T TYPE "P" INTO THE ADDRESS BAR, PLEASE DON'T TYPE "P" INTO THE ADDRESS BAR.
...P...
...ORNFREAKS.COM. OH! YOU'VE ALREADY GOT IT HERE! GOOD JOB, SON!

An Alternative Mission

Perhaps you read the last section and stammered out loud, "I can't bear to be the George to my teen's dragon." That sounds like something you'd say. After all, being a strict parent is for quadrilaterals with four equal sides. You'd much rather be Kidz Bop than Bad Cop. While your parental peers are desperately trying to snap their fingers in "kool" ways like anxious chimpanzees trying to catch supersonic fruit flies to impress their head-shaking adolescents, you know exactly what all the cool teens are digging. They're digging their hands deep into their pants. Use this nugget to your advantage in order to gain "cool pops" brownie points with your boy.

The next time you hear the dull, familiar, repeating thud of the bedpost thumping against the wall in your teen's room, cast doubt behind you like a toxic wedding bouquet. Kick that bedroom door down with all the excitement you can muster, and loudly proclaim your own enthusiasm for frantically pulling your tallywhacker as if to encourage a giant spider to escape from it. Give your "coming of age" man a big two thumbs up for rubbing one out, and offer to pass down to him your most prized X-rated celluloids like you would your collection of water-damaged Hall & Oates vinyl. Your son will no doubt be thrilled by your cavalier attitude towards painting the ceiling, and undoubtedly be moved by your offer to open up a joint account down at the wank bank.

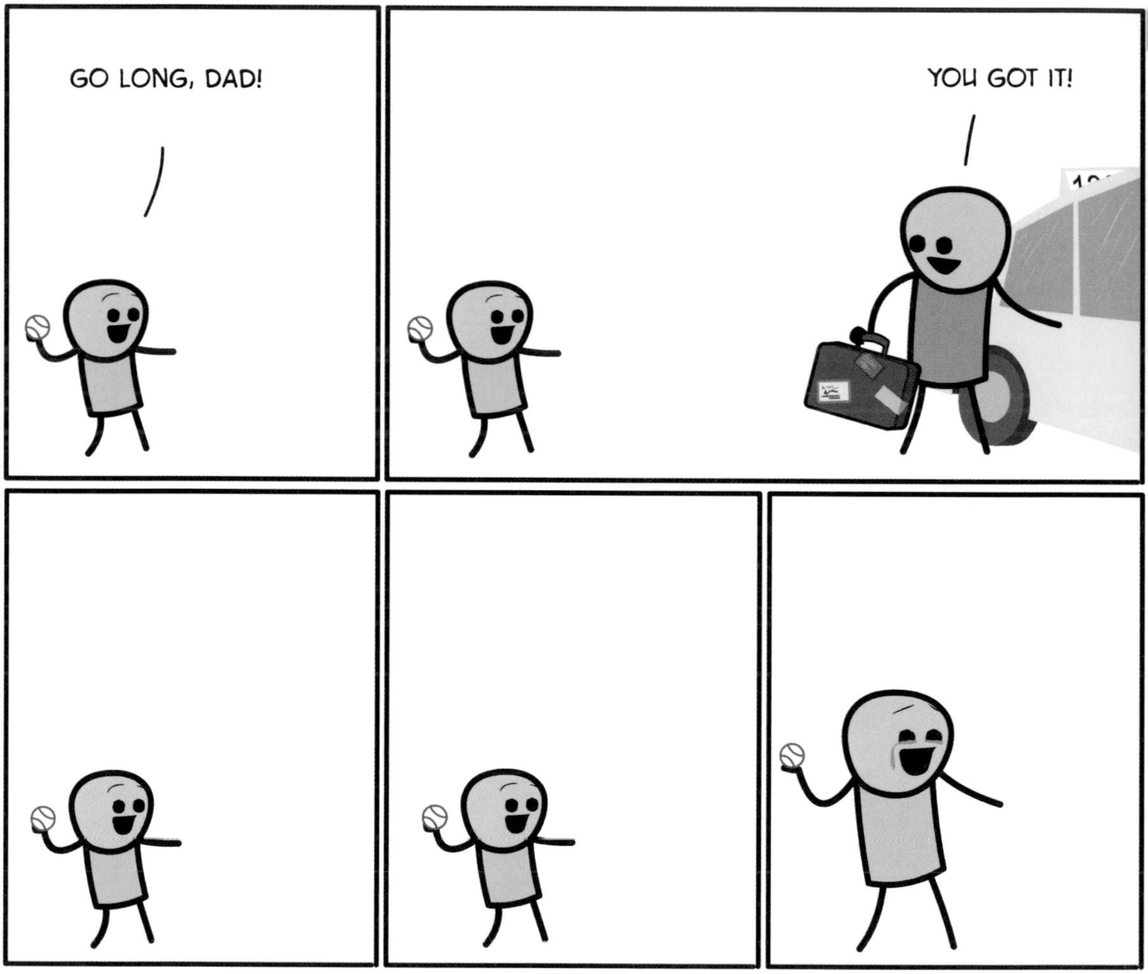
GO LONG, DAD!
YOU GOT IT!

Going Long

I can see it in your eyes.

You've peered at the accompanying illustration, and now you are heaving hay bales of secondary doubt onto the lurid, manure-stained trailer that is your domestic life. You used to spend your hard-earned money on long nights with the boys, liquored to the max, joyously pissing it up against the wall in some shoebox alleyway after the pub had long closed for the evening. Now you spend it all on apple juice for your sprog, yet it still gets pissed up the wall. Your wall. Cake-like, primary-colored vomit strewn throughout the darkest recesses of your house like some Easter omelette hunt, brings not anger to your forefront, but jealousy. That could've been your spew after the best night out of your life, a life now relegated to the back bench, after a quick substitution with your child in the first quarter of this big b-ball game we call happiness.

Enough with the metaphors, you might say. Whilst I can't guarantee that there won't be more, I can implore you to do this: walk out that door right now. Go get your life back. Get the boys back together. Piss on some leaves. Pump Ratt up to 11. Go be the loser you always wanted to be.

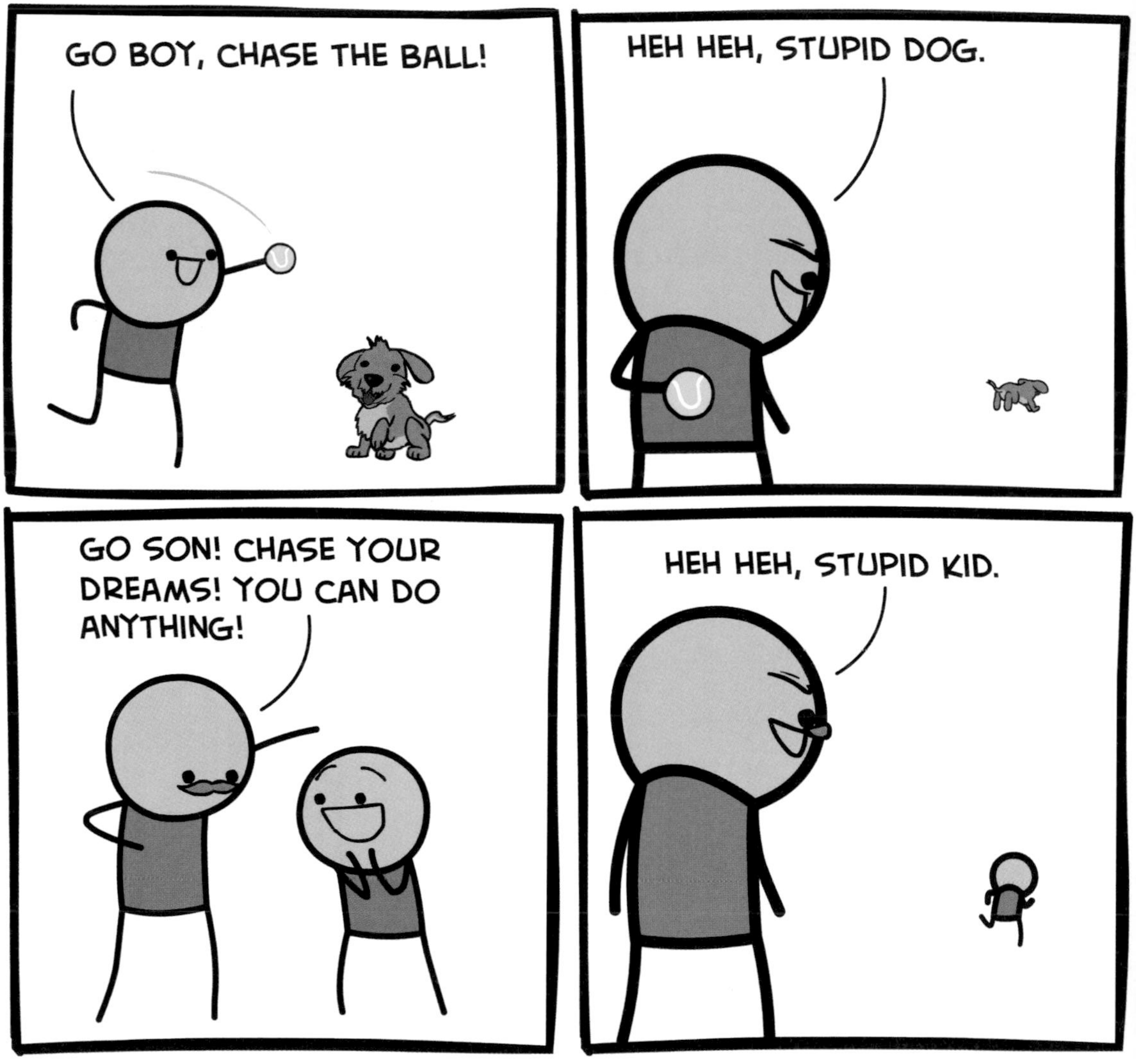
GO BOY, CHASE THE BALL!
HEH HEH, STUPID DOG.
GO SON! CHASE YOUR DREAMS! YOU CAN DO ANYTHING!
HEH HEH, STUPID KID.

Practice

Your sprog stares up at you as you lament. All you ever wanted was a dog. Your spouse suggested you get a child as a "practice dog," and so here you are, staring solemnly into the eyes of that decision. So do it. Practice. Feed your child nothing but kibble. Vigorously train them to shit outside. Have them beg for scraps at the table. Teach them all sorts of humiliating tricks. Prove to your spouse that you'd make a fantastic dog owner.

If you're fortunate, before long CPS will arrive at the door, congratulating you on your dog-owning prowess. "You've proven your worth," they will say, before pinning a small medal to your sweater and taking your practice dog to the nearest pound, freeing up your living space for the canine companion you've always wanted. Victory!

Unfortunately, when your dog arrives, it demands to be clothed, play your PlayStation, and sit at the table during dinner where it'll only eat mac and cheese. You hadn't prepared for this. Drat.

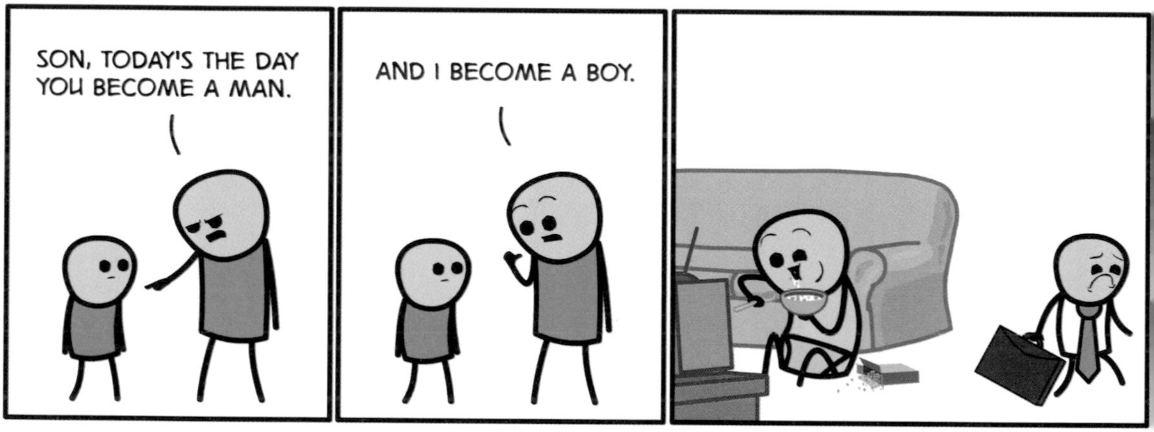
SON, TODAY'S THE DAY YOU BECOME A MAN.
AND I BECOME A BOY.

Living Vicariously

Many parents relive their childhood vicariously through their children, so why not take it a step further? Make a wee-wee in your pants. Wolf down that baby mush. Do a dirty little poo in your hand and slap it on the door. Run in fast, tight circles while loud cartoons blare from the TV like a belly-laughing thundercloud. Have your spouse join in on the reminiscing. It's now your child's obligation to pick up the slack around here, because who's going to be the grown-up of the house while you and your spouse are indulging in being proxy-childhood-having, be-diapered, babbling babybeasts? Certainly not you. Besides, this is all just practice for when you're older. Don't revert. Your child needs to grow up. Right now.

If your kid fails to immediately man/woman up and get a job like a contributing member of society (there's mouths to feed in this house, damnit), then call CPS and tell them your sob story. Inform them of how your child is horrifically neglecting you. Maybe they'll come to your aid and take you away to a nice, nuclear, loving home where you can be heaped with the kind of attention and nurturing you deserve.

Good grief, your child was a monster. I can't imagine how any decent child could treat a sweet, innocent man-baby like they did.

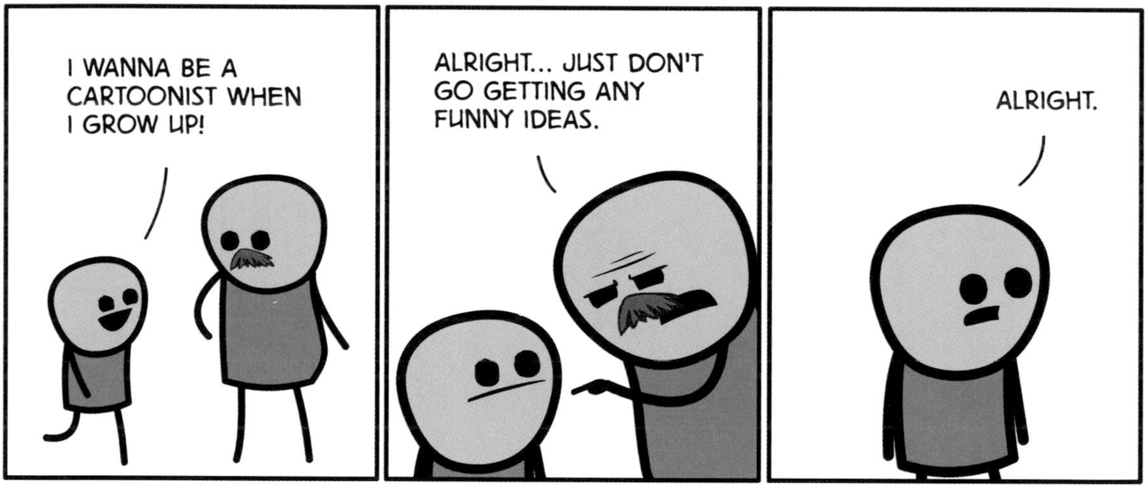
I WANNA BE A CARTOONIST WHEN I GROW UP!
ALRIGHT... JUST DON'T GO GETTING ANY FUNNY IDEAS.
ALRIGHT.

Nothing to See Here

No jokes here.

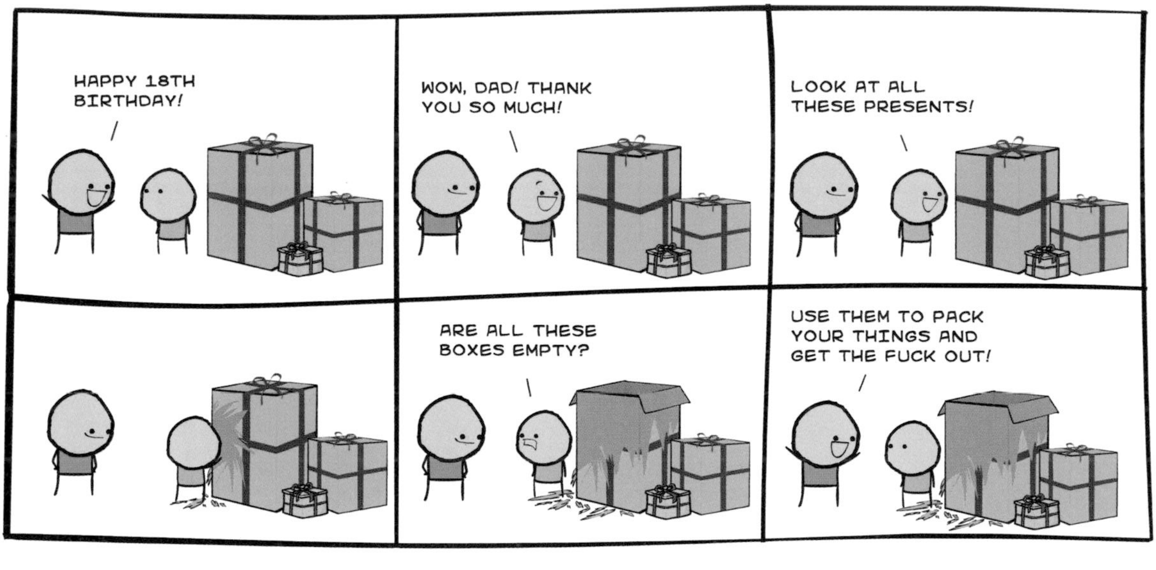
HAPPY 18TH BIRTHDAY!
WOW, DAD! THANK YOU SO MUCH!
LOOK AT ALL THESE PRESENTS!
ARE ALL THESE BOXES EMPTY?
USE THEM TO PACK YOUR THINGS AND GET THE FUCK OUT!

A Cardboard Odyssey

Children are the masters of the universe below our big grown-up knees. To the adult eye, the underside of a couch may be just that. To the imagination of a child, however, it may be a secret cave, castle—or indeed, my particular favorite after my father downed a few scotches—a bunker. Children gaze upon our towering adult frames with a mixture of awe and disgust, as if to stare onto The Gates of Argonath, were they built from subcutaneous fat and self-loathing. Our domestic world provides portals to entirely new worlds for our children, like some nebulous Lovecraftian nightmare.

Who cannot claim to hold a joyous memory of a time they were bestowed a gift, yet found the promise of converting the ginormous cardboard packaging into a parchment palace of sanctuary more diverting? Even in adulthood, some find it hard to unshackle themselves from the adrenaline rush. So strong was the longing my father still held for such memories, he spent two whole years in a cardboard box outside a local supermarket. He never desired much of anything else—all he ever asked for was a bottle of vodka and the occasional sandwich. So go on. Give that kid a big ol' cardboard box. Give him the life my father had.

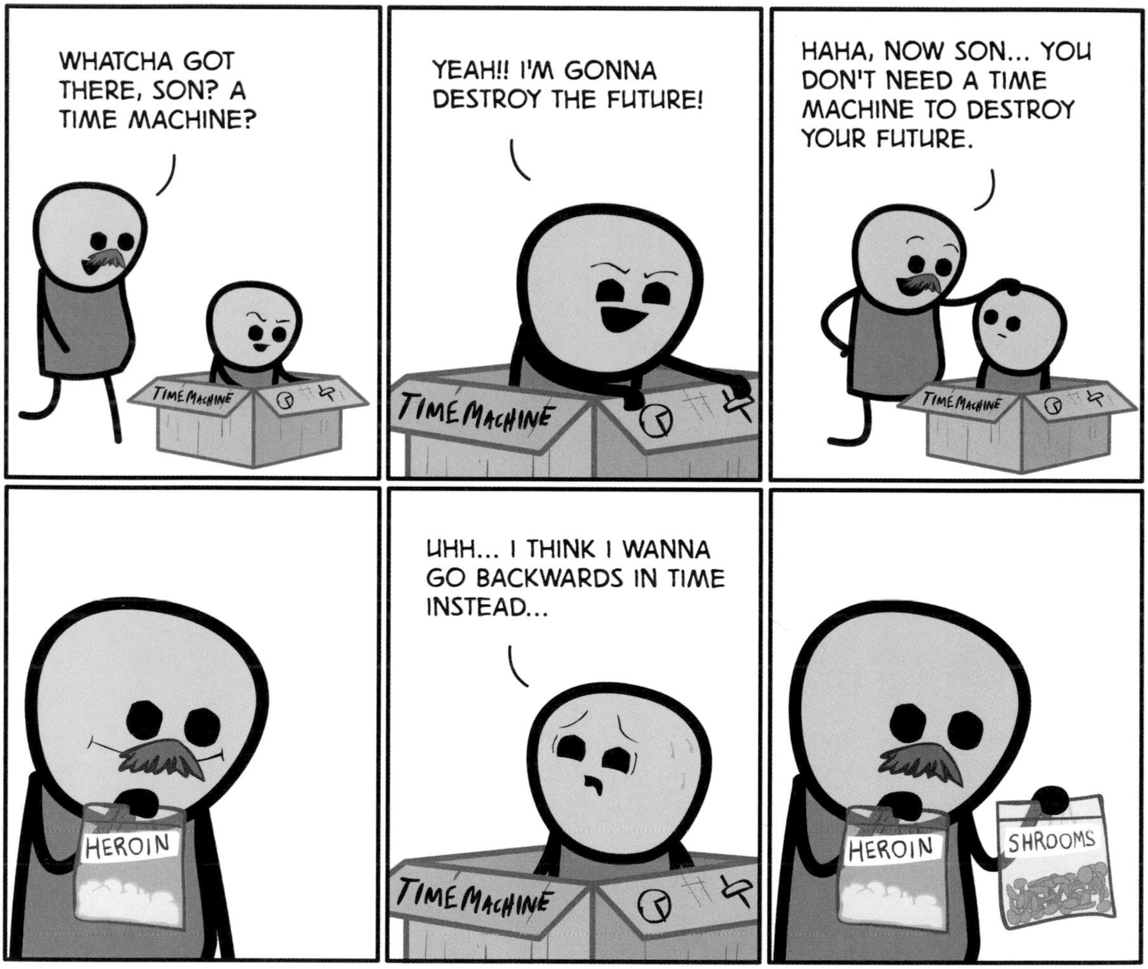
WHATCHA GOT THERE, SON? A TIME MACHINE?
TIME MACHINE
YEAH!! I'M GONNA DESTROY THE FUTURE!
TIME MACHINE
HAHA, NOW SON... YOU DON'T NEED A TIME MACHINE TO DESTROY YOUR FUTURE.
TIME MACHINE
HEROIN
UHH... I THINK I WANNA GO BACKWARDS IN TIME INSTEAD...
TIME MACHINE
HEROIN
SHROOMS

Fate

You'd better have listened to my advice in the last section, mister, because this section is all about the possibilities bestowed upon your child AFTER having given them a large cardboard box. If you haven't read the last section, I suggest you do now. I'll still be here.

Ready? Splendid. Having now blasted your blithering blighter with a hot slab of thick cardboard oblong, study their next move carefully. If they fashion it into a makeshift time machine, then there are one of two projections to be made. One, your child is an astute scientist in the making, ready to make the imponderable a reality. Two, your child is a fucking idiot, who genuinely believes cardboard will allow him to casually destroy all laws of physics and treat the sands of time like the London tube. Either way, your child has no need for a time machine when every question they could pose about their future can be answered by staring deep into your faint, distant eyes, or surveying the derelict, vast landscape of your gelatinous gut like some sort of frowning sunset. You will one day be this child's miserable past as well. You are the key keeper of their queries.

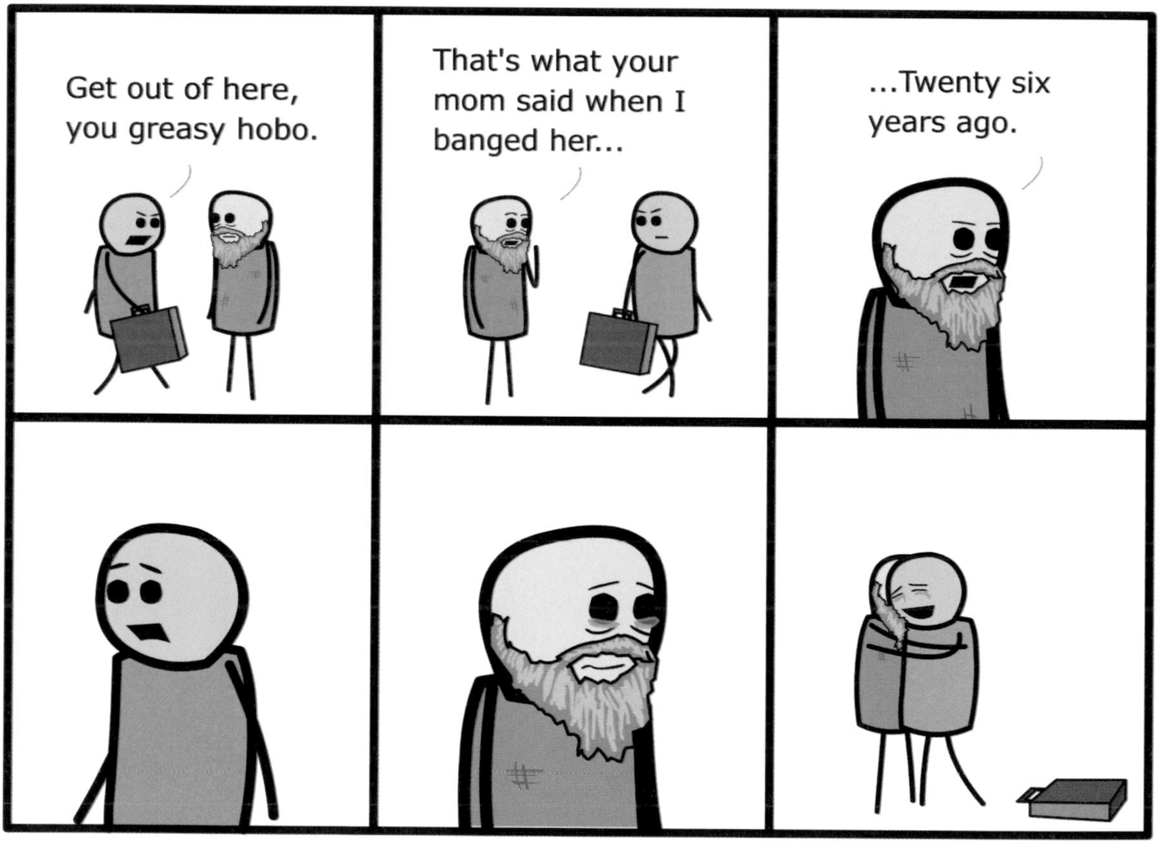
Get out of here, you greasy hobo.
That's what your mom said when I banged her...
...Twenty six years ago.

It's You

You're probably reading the accompanying illustration and thinking, "I'm obviously the successful young man with the briefcase and will receive advice based on that predication," but nope. You're the greasy hobo in this scenario. You are seven shades of disgusting. Your hair has the consistency of a trawler's net re-purposed to capture volcanic ash. Your beard is wild, and not in some masculine, brawny, beefcake fashion. It sincerely looks like a drooling, delirious wild animal. Be it a stoat, or perhaps a meerkat, your beard should only command the attention of a hunting rifle, and someone desperate enough to taxidermy its head for their wall of oddities. The only saving grace is the vague shelter it provides for the curb-stomped kernels of corn that are your remaining teeth. Your clothes are haggard, as if you've collected the remaining pieces of an exploded dinghy originally made from used sachets of barbecue sauce and attached them to your spectral body. This entire gruesome garb is held together only by the sobbing sores that you've gained from scrapping with someone over an equally toothless comb covered in bird shit. Oh, and my advice to you?

Don't even talk to your son. Just leave him alone. You're not worth his time.

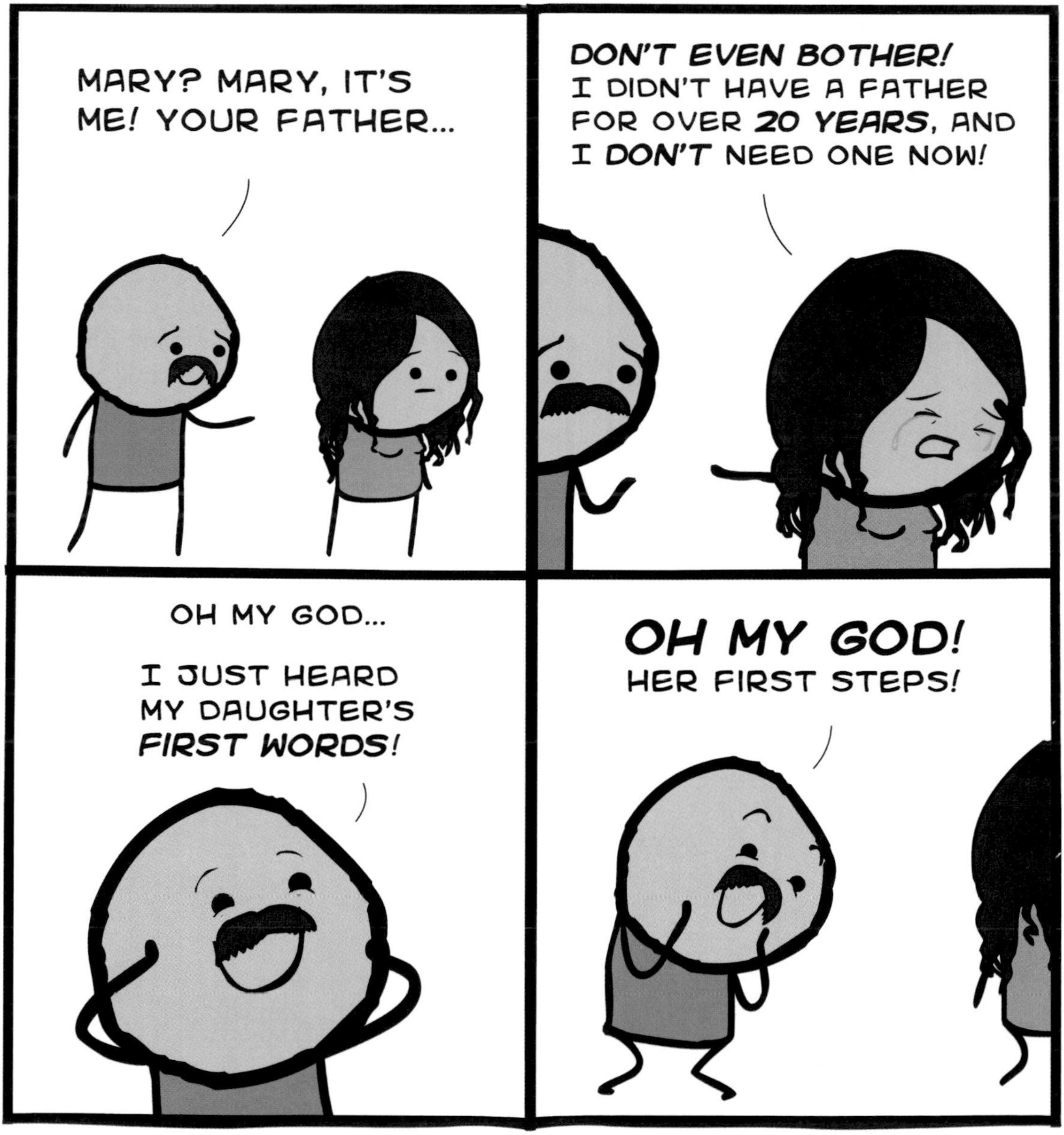
MARY? MARY, IT'S ME! YOUR FATHER...
DON'T EVEN BOTHER! I DIDN'T HAVE A FATHER FOR OVER 20 YEARS, AND I DON'T NEED ONE NOW!
OH MY GOD...
I JUST HEARD MY DAUGHTER'S FIRST WORDS!
OH MY GOD! HER FIRST STEPS!

Your Return

You've been gone for nigh over two decades on account of living in squalor, and now you want to re-enter your child's life like a meteor to their cozy stratosphere. Anticipate that your child may not be thrilled to see the haggard husk of half their origins, in the same manner they may never want to see the ashen remains of a burning car that they barely managed to escape. Instead, turn the bad feels 180 by giving them a non-low dose of hobo fomo.

"Where have you been?!" they may ask. "No, where the fuck have YOU been?!" should be your snappy response. After all, they've been missing out. You've spent the last two decades high as fuck on sweet drugs, having unprotected sex and generally being a careless miscreant. Could your child do any of that while they were at college? I think not. Taunt them about missing out on your rad life.

If you're lucky, they'll realize the error of their ways, and quickly pretend to jump with you into a pretend black Ford Mustang that you'd definitely own if you had any money, because you're a cool dad. Pretend Journey's "Be Good to Yourself" is playing on the pretend radio as you both run steadfastly into your new life of destitution.

TIDY YOUR ROOM AT ONCE!
I DON'T WANNA!
DON'T MAKE ME GET MY BELT!

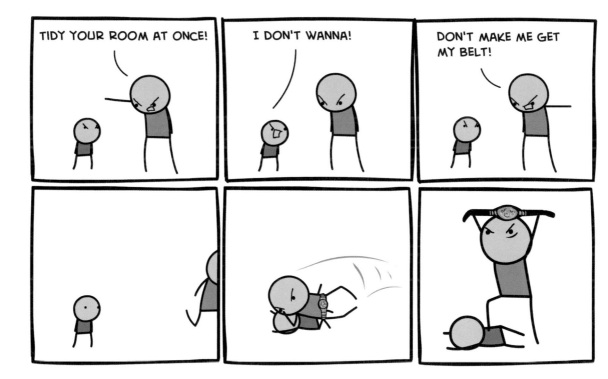

Playing the Heel

You enthusiastically watched pro wrestling as a youngun, yet somehow all that grapple knowledge hasn't come through for you. In between bouts of slamming fistfuls of lettuce into your basket at Kroger like it's a turnbuckle, and yelling into corn dogs like you're workin' the mic, you yearn for a new outlet for your squared circle savvy. Now you've got a sprightly youngster about the house, alongside a whole itinerary of awesome moves, holds, and suplexes that you've wanted to try out ever since you've found someone weenier than you. Why not try combining your lust for lariats with some tip-top parenting?

Powerbomb your kid into their clothes in the morning. Hurricanrana flip them steadfastly into bed at night. Chokeslam their face into some chicken nuggets. Fuck it, wear bright colored spandex and a pink cowboy hat. Your kid will think you're a goddamn superhero. A superhero that personally kicks the crap out of them at every opportunity, like they're some sort of villain. That'll give them character.

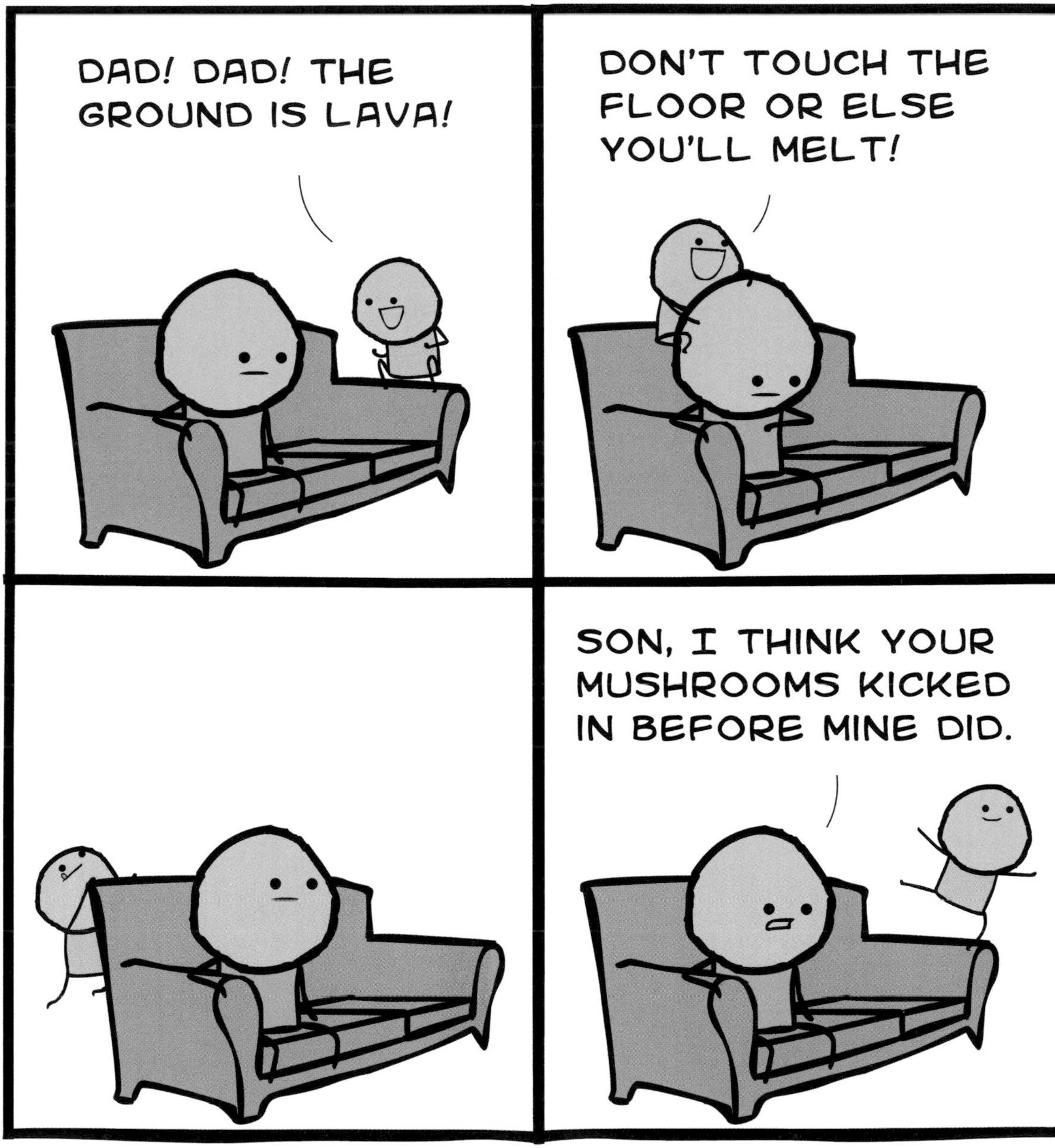
DAD! DAD! THE GROUND IS LAVA!
DON'T TOUCH THE FLOOR OR ELSE YOU'LL MELT!
SON, I THINK YOUR MUSHROOMS KICKED IN BEFORE MINE DID.

Dr. Doom-Little

Haha, look! Your kid's playing the fun "everything is lava" game! How adorable. But wait—that's a pretty pinpointed scenario for a child's innocuous playtime adventure. You might be chortling inattentively as your preschool protégé bounds between furniture like a self-operating whack-a-mole mallet, but they may know more than they're letting on. Your young one may already be practicing a safety drill in anticipation of a fiery disaster waiting to happen; perhaps part of a wider plot so diabolical that Ivan the Terrible wouldn't write it on the bathroom stall door as he's doing terrible twos. Is your child a mega villain in the works?

Lift your legs up immediately. Are your feet roaring with flames like they've both been on a couple's retreat to Hades? If not, you've escaped this time, but beware. Squint at your child hard, like you're afraid of your eyes falling onto the floor. Let them know with one glance that you are the Bond to their SPECTRE. They might even have already built some wiggy lair in a volcano. That'd explain the lava obsession.

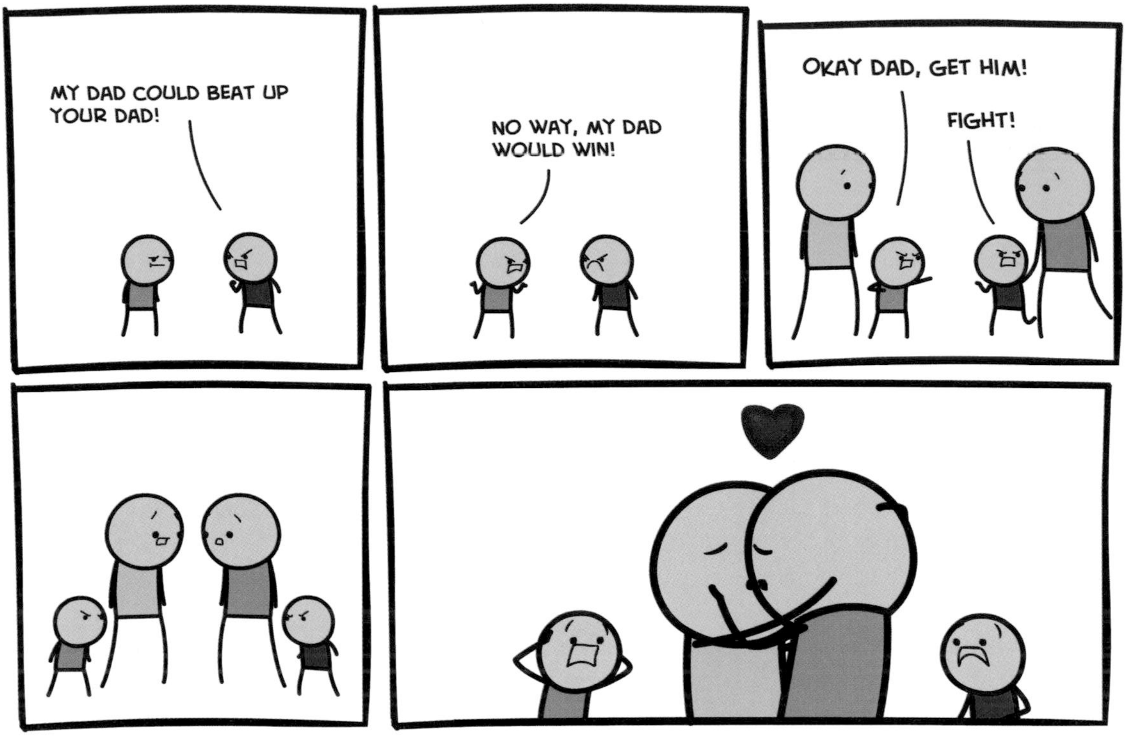
MY DAD COULD BEAT UP YOUR DAD!
NO WAY, MY DAD WOULD WIN!
OKAY DAD, GET HIM!
FIGHT!

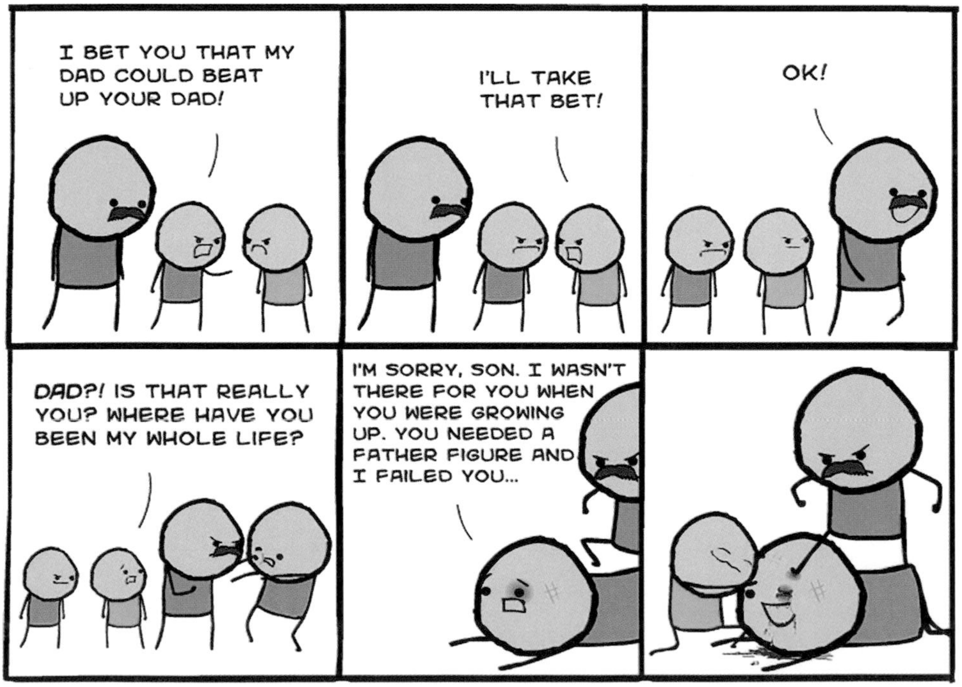
I BET YOU THAT MY DAD COULD BEAT UP YOUR DAD!
I'LL TAKE THAT BET!
OK!
DAD?! IS THAT REALLY YOU? WHERE HAVE YOU BEEN MY WHOLE LIFE?
I'M SORRY, SON. I WASN'T THERE FOR YOU WHEN YOU WERE GROWING UP. YOU NEEDED A FATHER FIGURE AND I FAILED YOU...

Smack My Dad Up

You didn't sign up for this at dad college. In fact, you were only there to drink. Had you known that your child was going to parade you around like some sort of Pokémon, you might have taken up taekwondo had they offered classes there. Instead you left with the equivalent of an AB liberal arts degree. You're a goddamn Pidgey.

Your child has arranged for you to fight their friend's dad like they're the runners of some illegal ring. They're not even pissed at each other. There's no honor to defend. They've just decided to hold some sporting competition, only instead of fighting each other like the cowards they are, they've enlisted their brawniest adult man meats.

You reckon you can settle this out with mature discussion like adults do, but as soon as other dad shows up, he marches towards you and smacks you square in the speaker before you can stutter a sentence. Pow! It's super effective! His fist at hitting your face, that is, and your face at collecting the entire force of his fist. It's a reciprocal relationship they have, his fist and your face. You fall to the ground immediately and stay down like an opossum in a gunfight, hoping that your opponent will claim victory and leave your sorry ass be. Nope, he keeps wailing on you with his big steel toecaps. One time, two times, four more times. His own kid eventually starts weeping, pleading with him to leave you alone because you look like you're already dead.

Eventually giga-dad and his kid get into their car, leaving you to explain to your kid why you collapsed like a slinky in a black hole. Quick, use your Pokémon knowledge. You were charging up for your big move. You just had to wait four more turns.

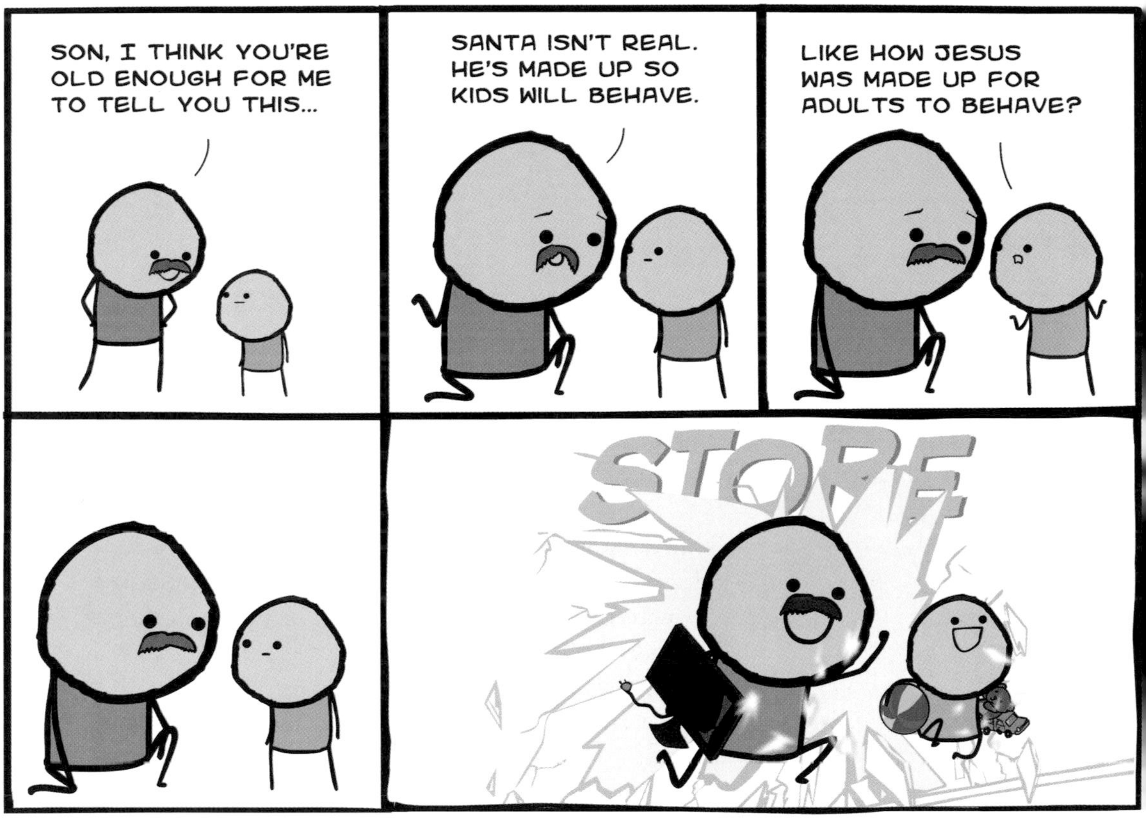
SON, I THINK YOU'RE OLD ENOUGH FOR ME TO TELL YOU THIS...
SANTA ISN'T REAL. HE'S MADE UP SO KIDS WILL BEHAVE.
LIKE HOW JESUS WAS MADE UP FOR ADULTS TO BEHAVE?
STORE

Let's Do a Christmas

Imagine the sound of sleigh bells ringing in the back of your mind as you read onward. Like any contemporary media worth its proverbial salt, this parenting book contains a bumper Christmas special section—and this is it. You're reading it right now. Put your feet in a hot bath of mulled wine, hang a yuletide bauble off your nose, and continue to read at a Christmas pace. Don't forget to ho ho first. Imparting a keen sense of decency upon your child is tough work, so why not pass the buck to a magical, obese, toy-making cryptid instead? If one isn't immediately coming to mind, let me give you a hint—it's Santa. Of course it's Santa, you bloody fool. Who else could teach your child wholesomeness quite like an odd-looking, bearded man, often found in the corner of a mall? One that insists that small children sit on his lap?

As we all know, morality is transactional. Like a seedy Six Flags shooting gallery, Santa will trade in well-aimed bullets of good character for the oversized teddy bear of . . . well, toys. Perhaps literally an oversized teddy bear. What your child receives from Santa is completely up to your discretion based on the yearly review you give to your child like they're your plebeian office drone. You are the judge, jury, and executioner of your child's festive happiness.

If you are of the practicing Christian flavor, whilst your baby is carefully managing their sense of morality by looking up to an old man, you yourself are managing yours by looking up to a 2000+ year-old baby. A baby that, in fact, grew up to be so powerful that if you don't receive his blessing before you pass away, you will be sent to the communal fire rave that is Hell for all eternity. A morally dubious power in itself. The question remains—where was Jesus's Santa? Who taught him morality as a child?

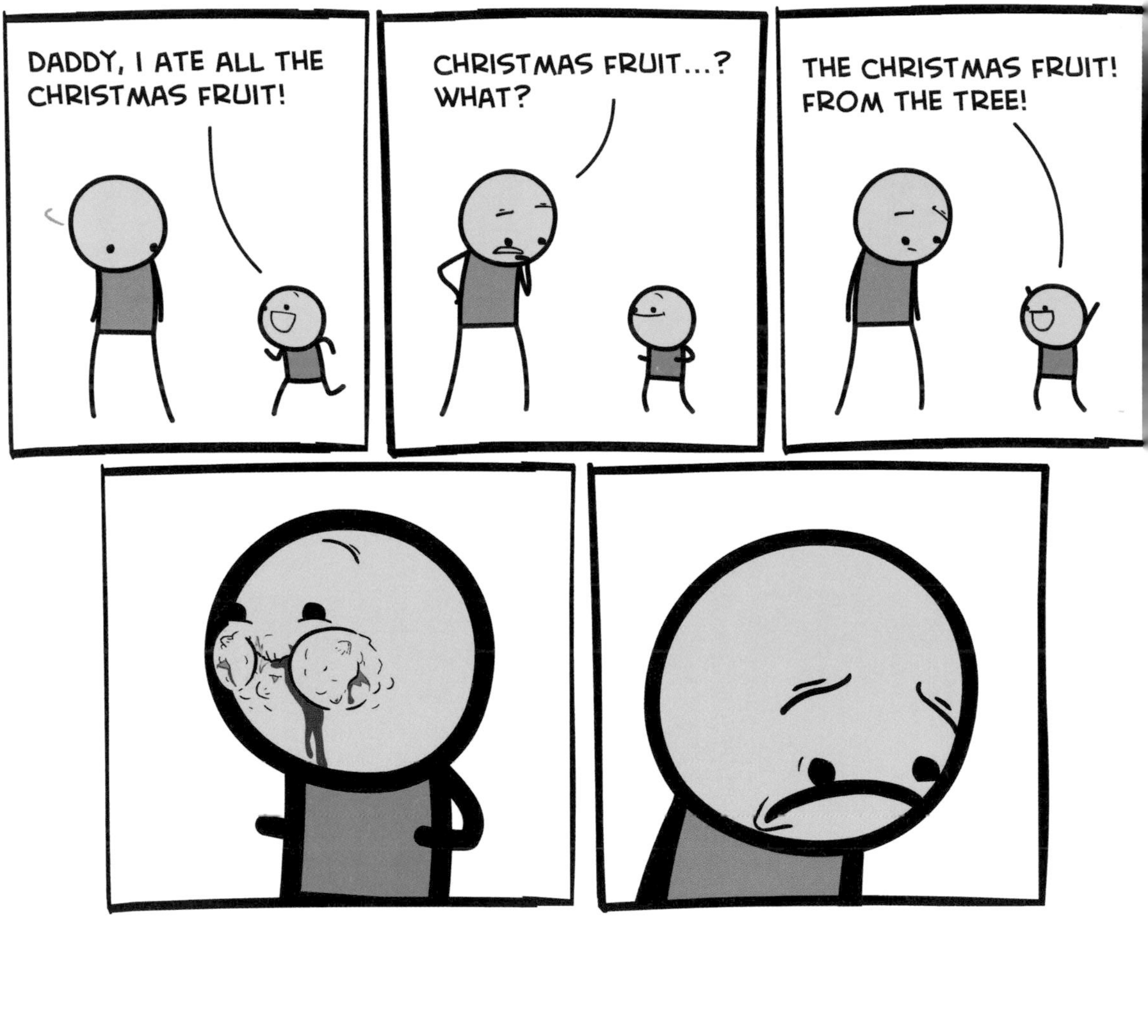
DADDY, I ATE ALL THE CHRISTMAS FRUIT!
CHRISTMAS FRUIT...? WHAT?
THE CHRISTMAS FRUIT! FROM THE TREE!

Suck It Up

An infant's mouth is an insatiable hoover-hole that will, despite possessing a strong distaste for any cuisine you offer besides mac and cheese, gobble up the nearest unmentionable, potentially fatal, horror like a lemming trying to swallow the edge of a cliff. Be it scum on the floor, muck in the garden, the tiniest parts of any remotely sophisticated device, or boogers in a nose (yours or theirs), children do not discriminate. They see with their mouth. So fuck it. Go ahead, let them do it.

Now you can spend that $100 you were saving up for a Roomba on cookie dough and balaclavas. Suddenly, the scum on the bathroom wall is gone, there's fewer spiders in the garden, and you're able to breathe more freely from your nose, though now you have to contend with a 56-piece orchestra's worth of shit and vomit all over the floor. Good job, now your house resembles a curd-like biotope of a Floridian swamp in the dead of summer. You really should've seen that coming. I don't know why you listen to me.

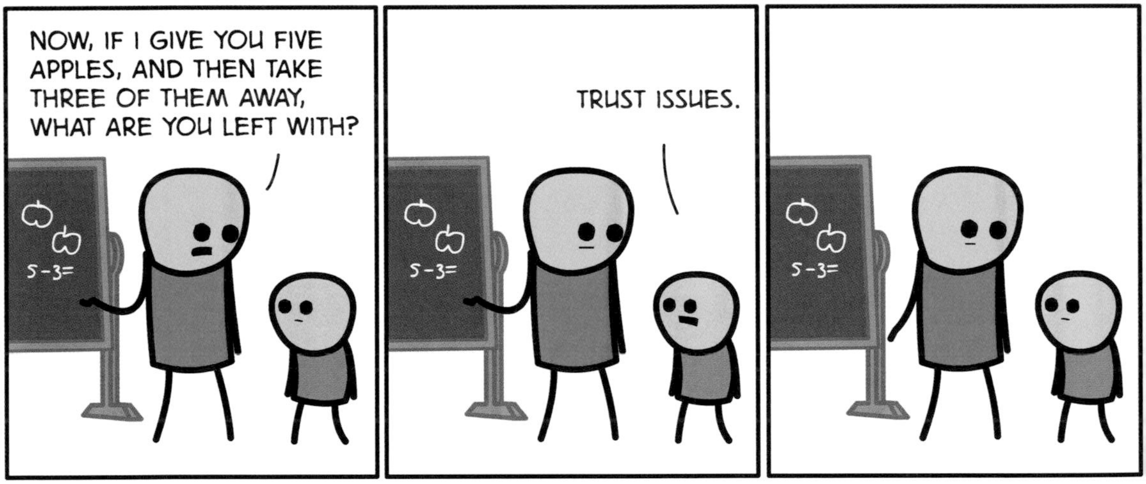
5-3=
NOW, IF I GIVE YOU FIVE APPLES, AND THEN TAKE THREE OF THEM AWAY, WHAT ARE YOU LEFT WITH?
5-3=
TRUST ISSUES.
5-3=

Apples

A is for apple. B is for bastard. If you take apples away from kids, you are an apple bastard.

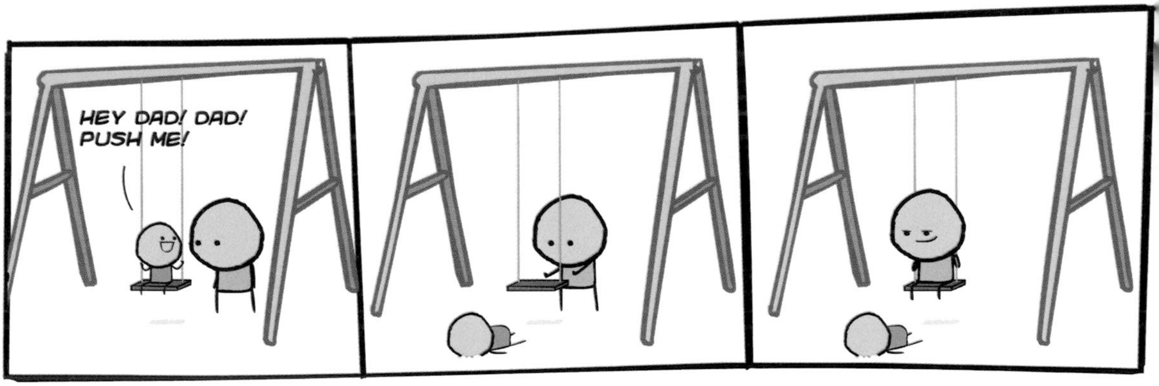
HEY DAD! DAD!
PUSH ME!

Push Me

"Push me," your child insists loudly, using all of his lung airs. That's a pretty vague request from a child on a swing. What do they mean? Perhaps they want you to test their patience? Perhaps they're insisting that you push them out of your life? Try number 1 first. Chide your child. Give them double wet willies so severe it feels like two seals desperately trying to escape from an orca by scrambling into their ears. Spit hard rages of ptooie into their hair. If this indeed enrages your child, you can now sleuthly segue into number 2.

Halt your child's protestations with a quick finger on their lips. Bear down on them. Feign crocodile tears like a crocodile who's just found out that an old high school nemesis has died. Tell them all about how you have had it up to "here" with their attitude, reaching aloft with your hand to denote the exact whereabouts of "here." It could be anywhere, that's up to you. You know your child best, so you should know the full XYZ coordinates of "here" that will convey to your child the full severity of this situation. Now do a 180 and run like the heavens. If your child attempts to chase after you, mock his shrimpy stomps with a Vincent Price cackle as you gallop away like a gazelle competing at the Olympics. You are now free.

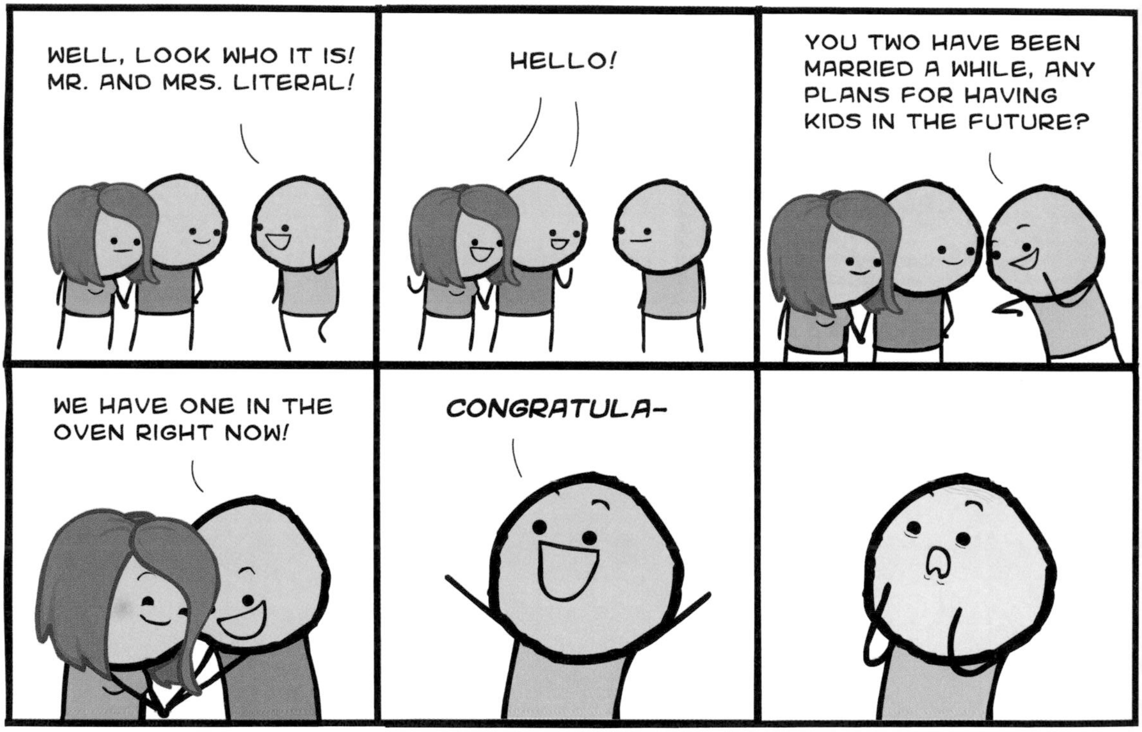
WELL, LOOK WHO IT IS! MR. AND MRS. LITERAL!
HELLO!
YOU TWO HAVE BEEN MARRIED A WHILE, ANY PLANS FOR HAVING KIDS IN THE FUTURE?
WE HAVE ONE IN THE OVEN RIGHT NOW!
CONGRATULA-

Cooking

It's certainly not advisable to eat your child. You're not a Scientologist, after all. However, there are other outlets for your strange, burning desire to combine good parenting with cooking. See the next section.

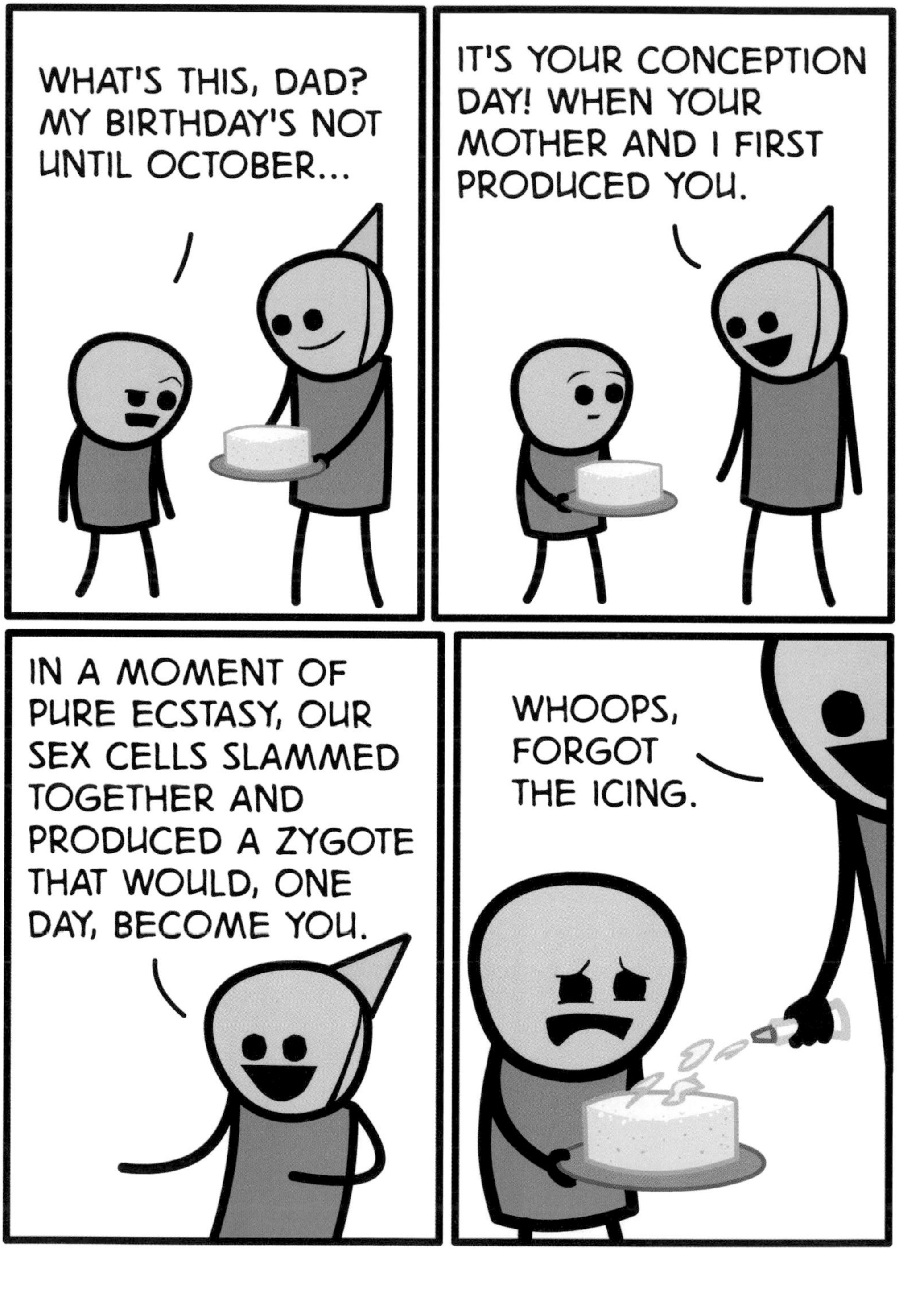
WHAT'S THIS, DAD? MY BIRTHDAY'S NOT UNTIL OCTOBER...
IT'S YOUR CONCEPTION DAY! WHEN YOUR MOTHER AND I FIRST PRODUCED YOU.
IN A MOMENT OF PURE ECSTASY, OUR SEX CELLS SLAMMED TOGETHER AND PRODUCED A ZYGOTE THAT WOULD, ONE DAY, BECOME YOU.
WHOOPS, FORGOT THE ICING.

A Recipe

Describing the finer points of sexual congress to your child can be taxing by itself. Instead, explain the complex relationship between birds and bees using this quick and easy recipe.

INGREDIENTS

2 beets
1 cheese-filled smoked sausage
2 slices of whole white bread
2 thick cut slices of honey-roasted ham lunch meat
2 tablespoons of garlic ranch
1 10 in. length of cooking twine
1 child (but you can add more if you want)

PREP TIME: About 30 seconds (knowing you)

COOKING TIME: 9 months

INSTRUCTIONS

1. Preheat oven to 400 °F.

2. Place the child beside you to observe what you are doing.

3. Thread twine through both beets from the top of each beet, tying them together closely. Thread both ends of twine through one end of the sausage and tie tightly together. Presentation is key in this recipe, so make sure it looks like a cock and balls. Prick a small hole in the end of the sausage, allowing a small sputter of cheese to drip out and onto the end lightly, like a butterfly's tear resting on a leaf.

(Continued on next page)

4. Apply one slice of the honey-roasted ham on top of one slice of white bread. Apply two tablespoons of garlic ranch on top of ham. Repeat with the remaining slices of bread and ham, then apply upside down on top. It should look like a ham sandwich. Right now, it is one.

5. Tenderly caress the ham sandwich, exploring the inside delicately with your touch. You don't want to hurt the sandwich, but you want to show that you are confident and assertive. Gently, sensually lick the crusts. Dance the tip of your tongue on the ham, alternating between quick flicks and slow, supple caresses. Get into a groove. Continue this for a few minutes until the sandwich is quivering in anticipation.

6. Now that your sandwich is prepared, reach for the sausage. Wrap your hand completely around it with self-assured intent. Let that sausage know who's in control. It's you. For once. Gently lick from the beets to the tip. Palpate the beets with your other hand delicately, as if to guess how many marbles are in a bag. Tease the sausage. Pull your head away and lick wildly around your mouth in a feral, animalistic fashion. Growl like a dog ripping apart a soft toy. You are a cheese-crazed guzzler. Give the length one last long lick before wrapping your smacker completely around the sausage. You are dangerous, and you mean business. Slide your moist muzzle along the meat pole. Look up to the ceiling, as if to beg for approval. Speed up your groove. You are the master of the sausage, and you will make it do your bidding. Increase your intensity. Build up steam. Slide up and down the bratwurst with the force and confident reliability of a powerful locomotive. Nothing can stop this train. You will be arriving at your destination soon.

7. When the time draws near, you'll know it. You've generated enough electricity within this sausage to power Gainsville, TX with your talented smacker. Here's the big moment! Release your mouth and aim the banger directly at the sandwich, squeezing hard to spurt the cheese all over the ham. In nothing but a suffocating flash, it is done. Slow down on the ecstasy, and deescalate the vibe. Now you've gone and made a mess. Sweaty and gaspless, try to slow your pounding heart. Then come to a thumping realization that hits hard in your stomach like you've swallowed a cannonball. You've gotten carried away. Again. Start to panic.

8. Hold your hands in your head and pace heavily, with big, freaked-out stomps. Try to reason   with the cheese-infused sandwich, "I couldn't stop!" "What does this mean?" "Do you think we'll be okay?" "I'm not ready for this!" Let the sandwich reassure you that while you should have paid more due care, you're probably safe. Wipe your sweaty, cold brow with a handful of relief, whilst still maintaining a degree of wariness that should haunt you for the next month or so.

9. In a penultimate fashion, bung all your food preparations hastily into some tinfoil and place in a tray. Insert into pre-heated oven and allow to cook for approximately 9 months.

10. Once the meal is fully cooked, pull hastily from the oven and slap onto the kitchen table in front of your child, pointing towards it as if to accuse him of the undelectable results. It should resemble a long-charred, pungent glimpse into what a natural disaster on Venus must look and smell like. Sternly bark at your child, "That's you. That's what you look like."

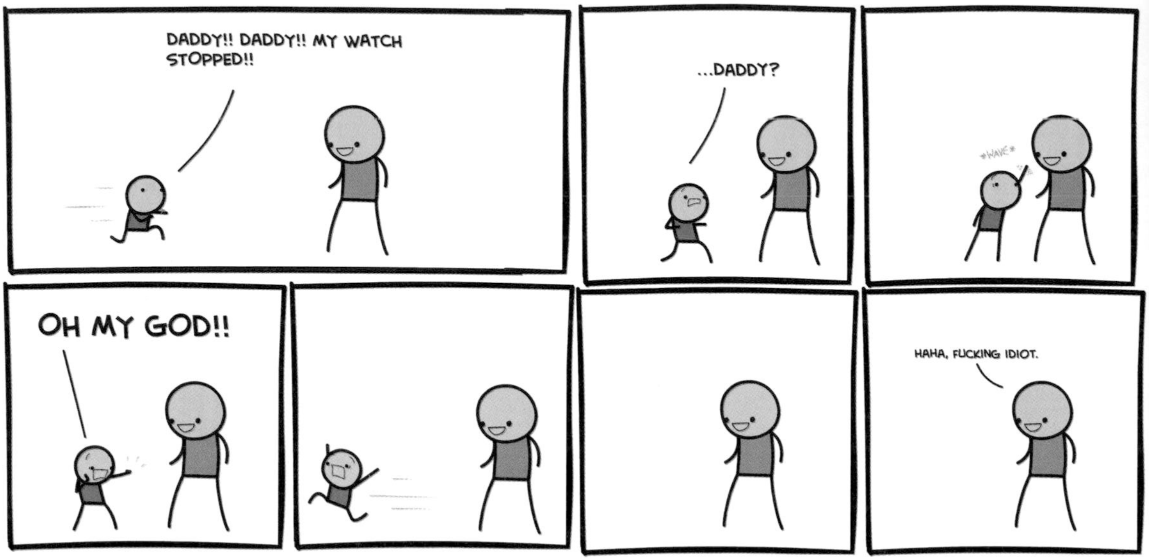
DADDY!! DADDY!! MY WATCH STOPPED!!
...DADDY?
WAVE
OH MY GOD!!
HAHA, FUCKING IDIOT.

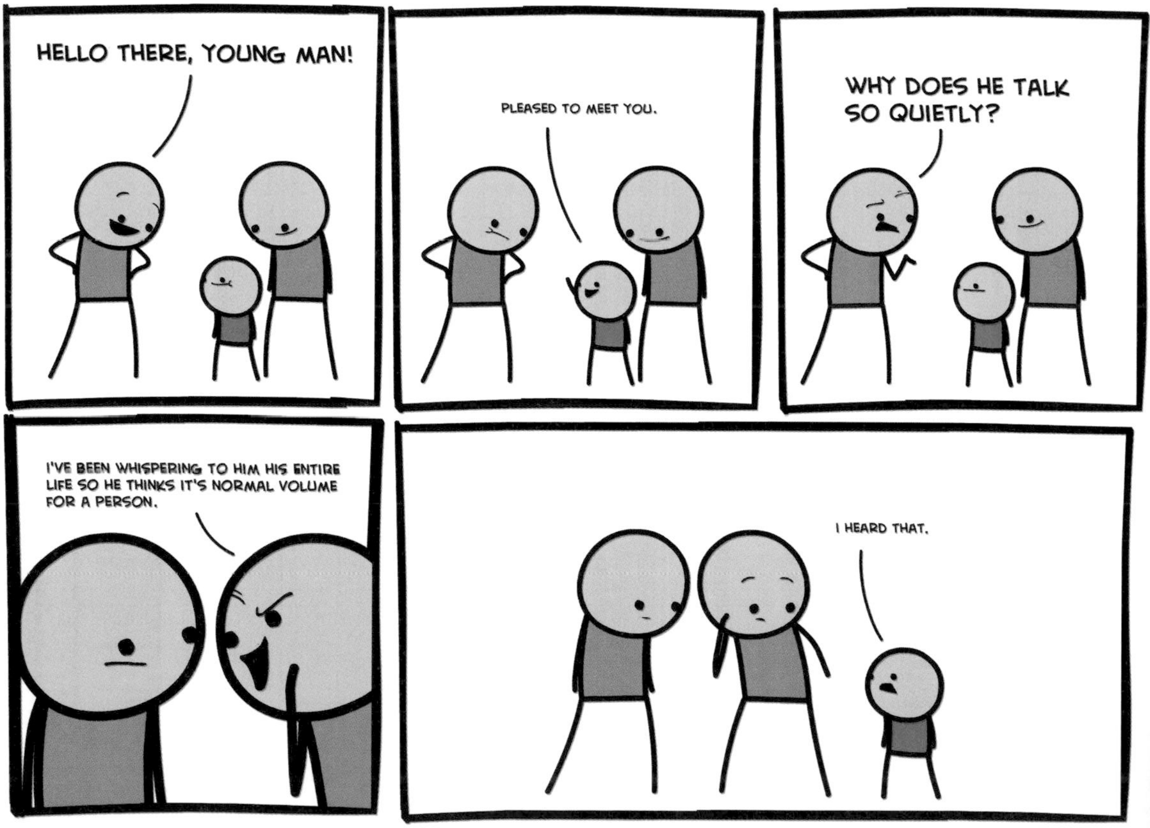
HELLO THERE, YOUNG MAN!
PLEASED TO MEET YOU.
WHY DOES HE TALK SO QUIETLY?
I'VE BEEN WHISPERING TO HIM HIS ENTIRE LIFE SO HE THINKS IT'S NORMAL VOLUME FOR A PERSON.
I HEARD THAT.

Dickery

You are the Morpheus to your child's Neo. Whilst I certainly don't recommend giving your child any non-FDA approved pills, you can still transmogrify the blank page that is their budding perception with all sorts of devious deception. Consider your child your personal petri dish. Not only are they a great place for cultivating all sorts of bacteria and disease, they are your personal lab for all sorts of fun human experimentation.

Lie to them from the beginning. Create a topsy-turvy world. The dog is a cat. Leaves grow on trees when they masturbate too much. Moths worship lamps because of their religious beliefs. The earth is flat. Russia had no part. Go crazy. Use your imagination.

Pack 'em full of misinformation like a lunchbox that's filled with concrete. On your kid's first day of school, step back, put your feet up, and enjoy the resulting carnage. Write down the results in a thesis for no one.

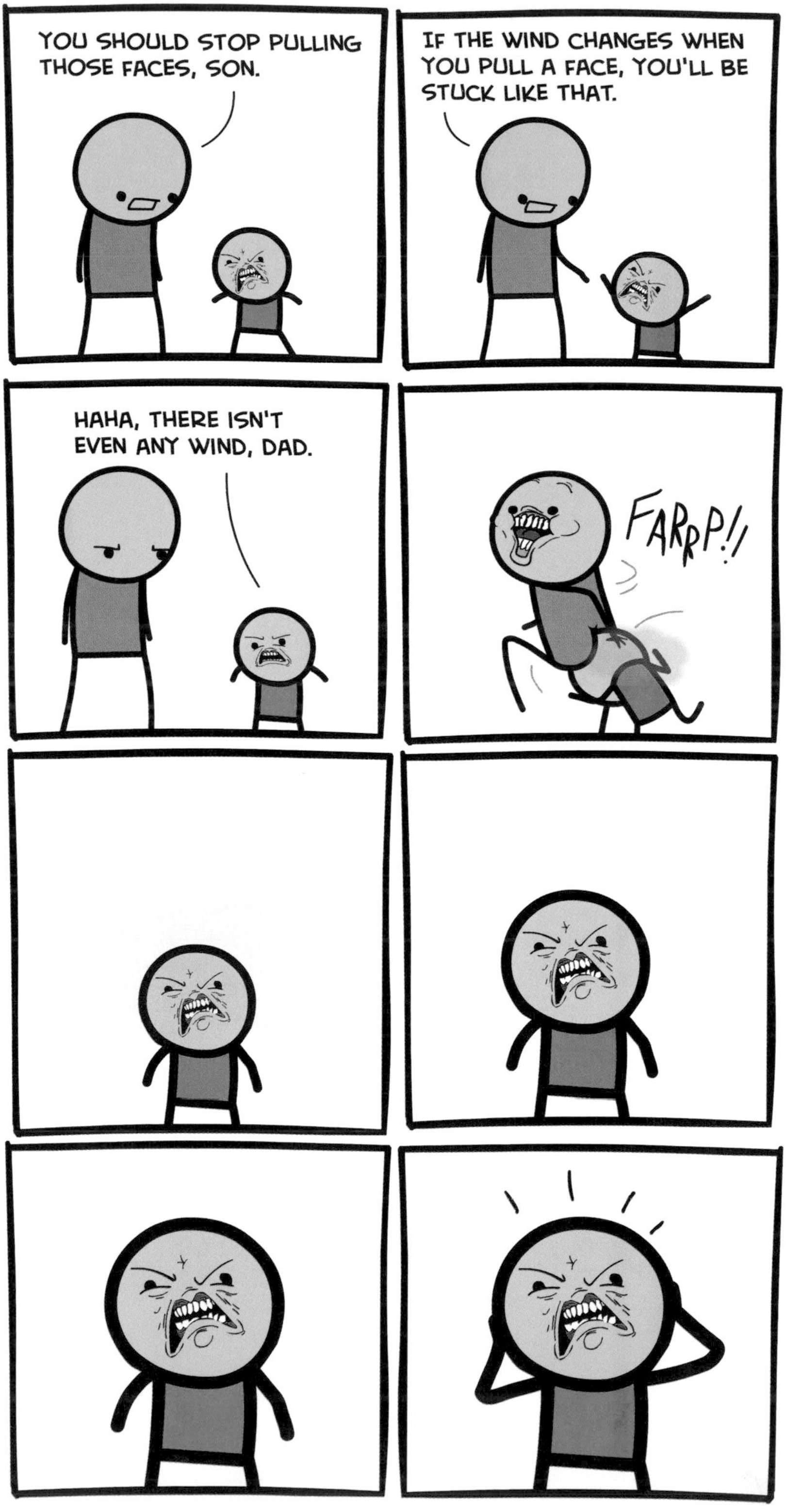
YOU SHOULD STOP PULLING THOSE FACES, SON.
IF THE WIND CHANGES WHEN YOU PULL A FACE, YOU'LL BE STUCK LIKE THAT.
HAHA, THERE ISN'T EVEN ANY WIND, DAD.
FARRP!!

Dickery For Dummies

You've read the last section and paused. "Whilst I'd love to try this out, I'm far too stupid to carry out such a long, sustained campaign of dickery," you mournfully whisper into your own ears. Never fear, for you have one long-proven trick up your sleeve. Or your arse. Consider it low-hanging fruit from your low-hanging bottom.

Fart on your kid at every opportunity. Clap huge, thunderous clouds of methane upon them like Zeus. Try it point-blank; press so close that your child looks like he's been kissed on the cheek by a lamprey wearing brown lipstick by the time you're done. Suspend arcs of farts from the floor to the ceiling of an entire room for your child to get trapped in, like you're some sort of massive fart spider. Treat it like sport. Reign from your throne of farts. Laugh diabolically. You're the king of France with flatulence. No thesis required.

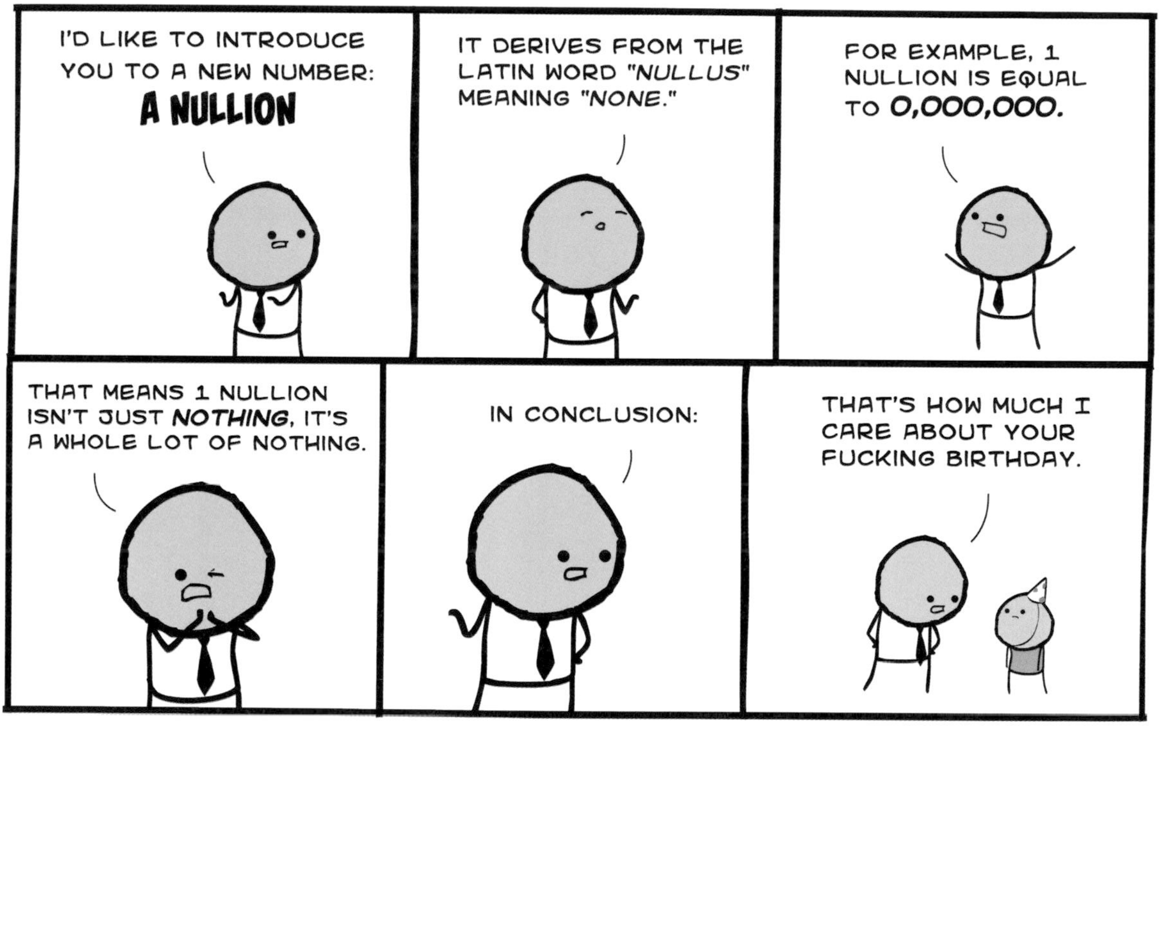
I'D LIKE TO INTRODUCE YOU TO A NEW NUMBER:
A NULLION
IT DERIVES FROM THE LATIN WORD "NULLUS" MEANING "NONE."
FOR EXAMPLE, 1 NULLION IS EQUAL TO 0,000,000.
THAT MEANS 1 NULLION ISN'T JUST NOTHING, IT'S A WHOLE LOT OF NOTHING.
IN CONCLUSION:
THAT'S HOW MUCH I CARE ABOUT YOUR FUCKING BIRTHDAY.

Birthday

Your infant demands undue reward for their being here today, ignorant to the labor that you and your spouse undertook in creating their smug, tomato-faced little fizzog. "I want big, expensive gifts! Lavish me with expensive gifts like I'm a cool fucking pharaoh!" they carp as they bang their bonce against the wall. That's your damn head. You built it, it's yours. It's time for them to respect your property, and to give credit where credit's due.

The true heroes of today are you and your spouse's assiduous genitals. Your child is riding off the sweat of their pubic brow like a trust-fund twerpazoid, keen to take the credit for your gonad's graft. Frame photographs of your dangly bits on the wall like portraits of a pompous, gauche third-world dictator. Do a military show of strength with your spouse, proudly marching through your living room with your parts as if to demonstrate to the entire world your fearsome firepower. Instead of giving your child gifts, make them say "thank you" repeatedly to both sets of your persevering privates as if they negotiated your child's freedom from a hostage situation carried out by a terrorist cell full of sharks. If they even dare to mention a gift on their birthday, remind them that you did indeed "make them with your dick." This is you and your spouse's day, after all. Let your glory reign supreme.

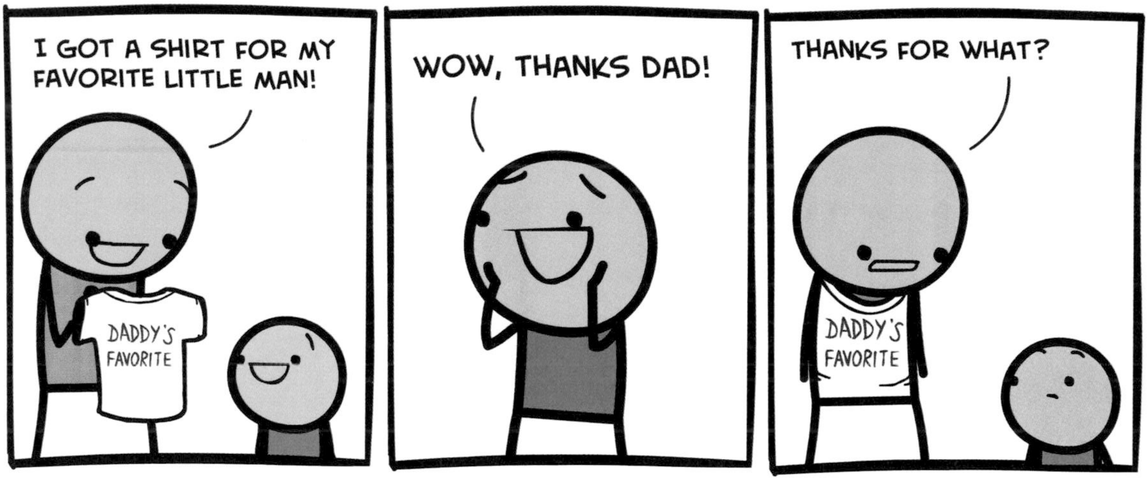
I GOT A SHIRT FOR MY FAVORITE LITTLE MAN!
DADDY'S FAVORITE
WOW, THANKS DAD!
THANKS FOR WHAT?
DADDY'S FAVORITE

Whose Favorite?

The yawning hole in your soul demands . . . approv . . . al? Your spouse would rather sit on a pepper dispenser than have sex with your saggy midriff. Your child writes your name in crayon and then runs it through the paper shredder in your office. Why's your kid anywhere near your paper shredder? That shit's dangerous for tiny tots. Oh right, your spouse. She's taught them how to use it with care in order to placate their burning eagerness to symbolically smite you.

You turn to your buddies at the bar. None of them want to have sex with you either, nor do they want to stop shredding your name. Desperate, you walk home surly and tipsy through the center of town with your arms hanging alongside your slumped head, like the two thieves to your Jesus. You pause outside a children's clothing store, which is open because it's 2:30pm. You squint into the window, perking up and slamming against it as you discover what seems to be the only plausible manifestation of your self-worth remaining. You peel your hands off and limp to the counter inside.

There, you ask a clearly uncomfortable clerk if the shirt in the window is available in an XXL size. "That's . . . one fat kid," the clerk mumbles. You realize her meaning, and woefully try to negotiate with the context of the situation. "Yes . . . I . . . have a very fat kid."

You stumble out the door, holding aloft your reused Kroger bag like a trophy. You get home and walk past the moans from the kitchen, and the intense buzzing from your office, to your bedroom. There, you stretch the shirt over your blimpy belly and stare in the mirror. "Daddy's favorite," it says. You giggle a little like a schoolgirl. You even consider tweaking your nipples a little before breaking down and crying.

This could be you. There is salvation.

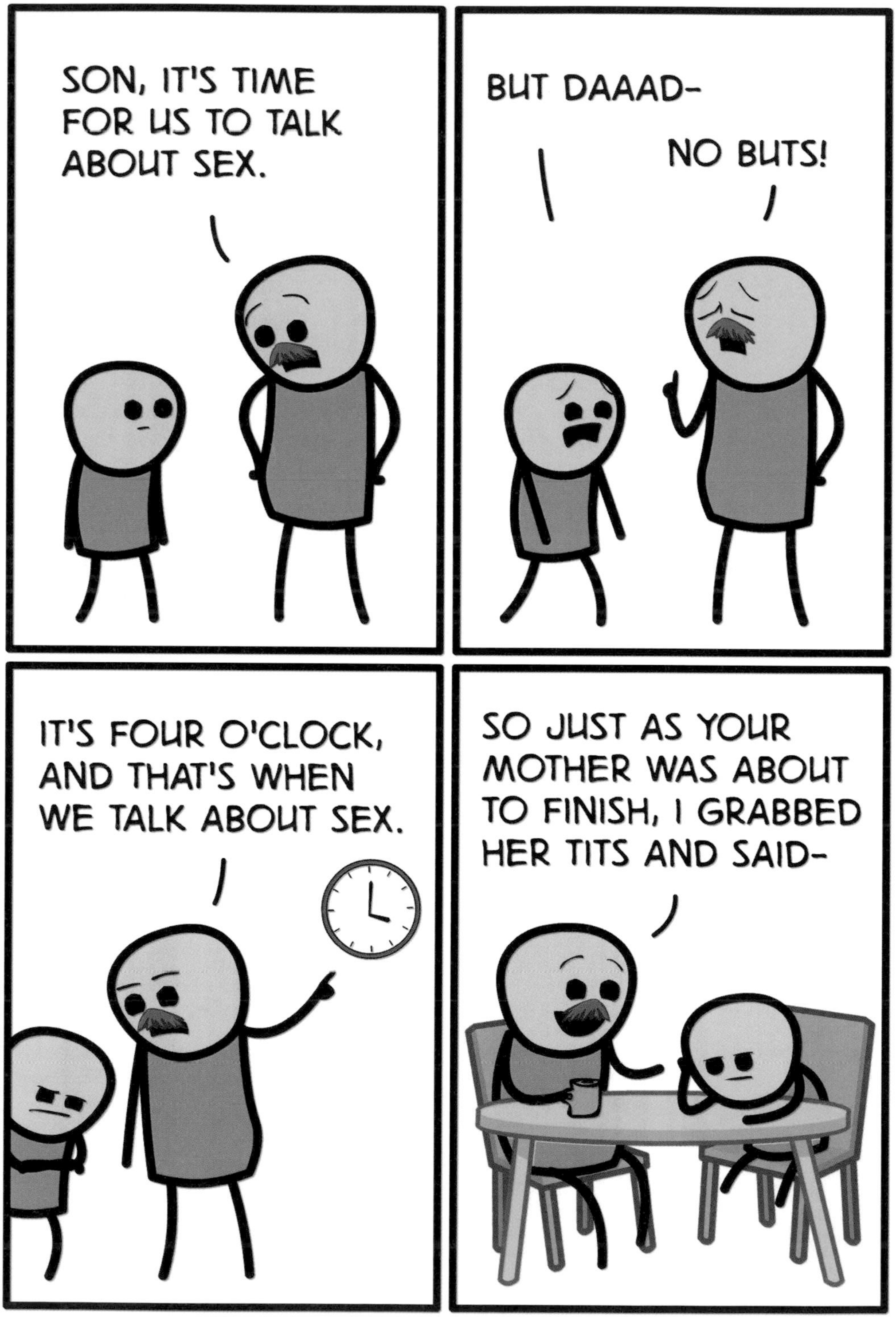
SON, IT'S TIME FOR US TO TALK ABOUT SEX.
BUT DAAAD-
NO BUTS!
IT'S FOUR O'CLOCK, AND THAT'S WHEN WE TALK ABOUT SEX.
SO JUST AS YOUR MOTHER WAS ABOUT TO FINISH, I GRABBED HER TITS AND SAID-

I'm a Cool Boy

Your child shakes their head as they stare at your orange crocs. Your cargo pants are mustard-stained and so alive with bacteria that they're ready to leap off your body to escape from the tenacious stench of body odor that trickles down from your inguinal region to your testicles, like blood from a long-dead animal. The Stone Temple Pilots shirt you bought 20 years ago now barely wraps around your pillowy gut like a condom trying to eat an ostrich egg. "What a bloaty boy," your child thinks, "how did he ever get laid?"

Tell him in great detail about how you got tail. Describe prudently all the areas of your spouse's body that you have explored. Your finger is Nathan Drake. Describe its adventures like one of grandpa's old war stories, except grandpa fought in 'Nam, so the stories have more in common on the face of it than you might expect. Describe the gore. The horrors. The spoils of sexy war. If your child is sane, they should curl up into a ball and immediately exit the room, rolling like a pillbug, unable to unhear your unspeakable speakables. Who's the cool boy now?

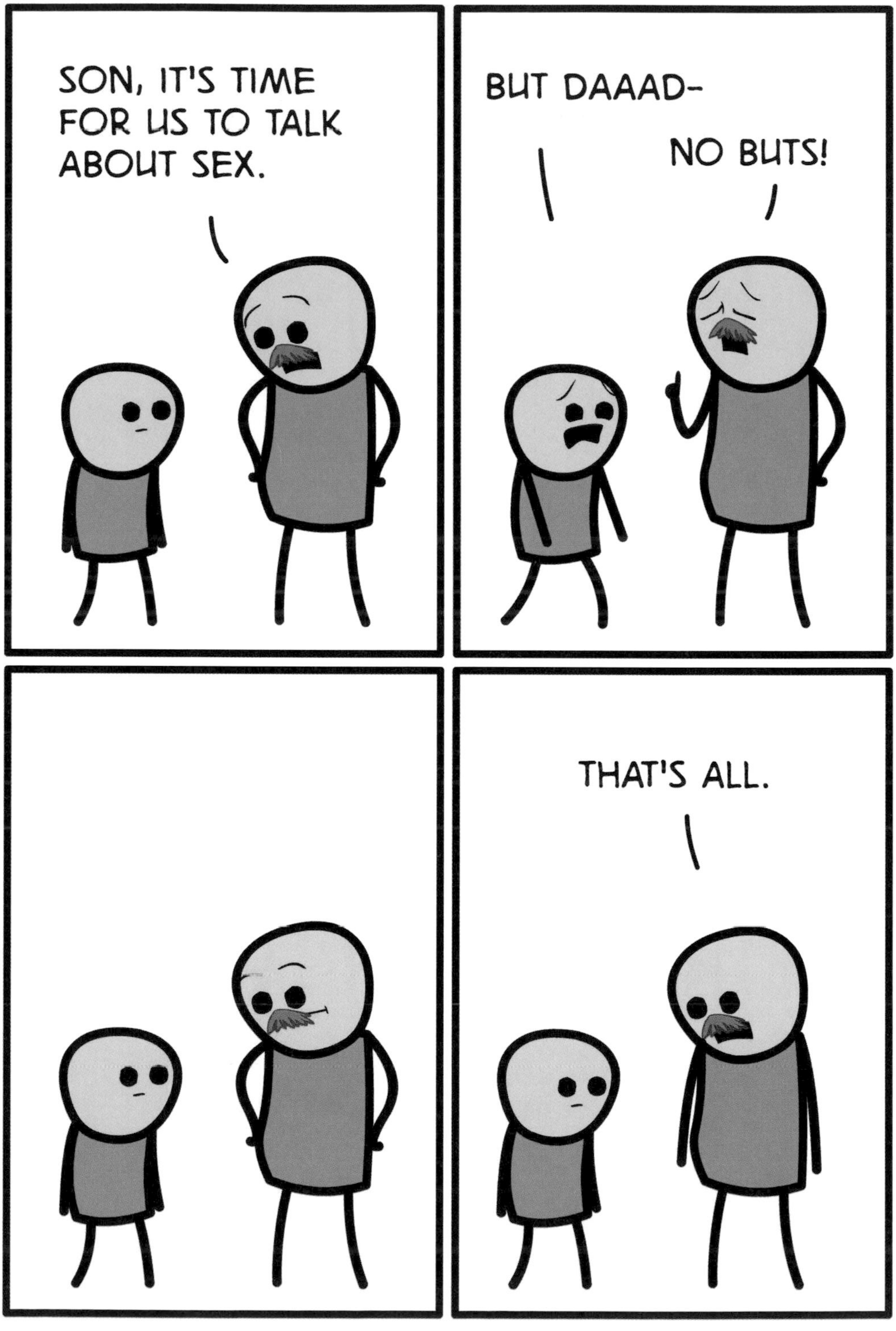
SON, IT'S TIME FOR US TO TALK ABOUT SEX.
BUT DAAAD-
NO BUTS!
THAT'S ALL.

I'm a Cool Boy 2

Don't talk about the arse.

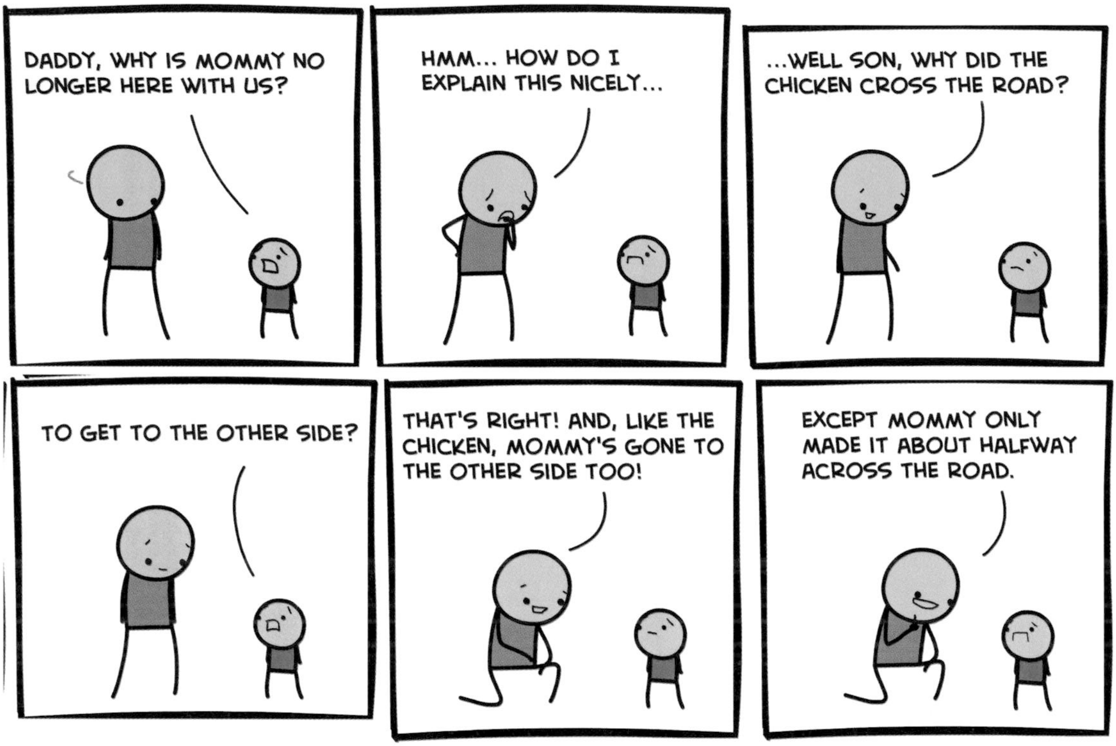
DADDY, WHY IS MOMMY NO LONGER HERE WITH US?
HMM... HOW DO I EXPLAIN THIS NICELY...
...WELL SON, WHY DID THE CHICKEN CROSS THE ROAD?
TO GET TO THE OTHER SIDE?
THAT'S RIGHT! AND, LIKE THE CHICKEN, MOMMY'S GONE TO THE OTHER SIDE TOO!
EXCEPT MOMMY ONLY MADE IT ABOUT HALFWAY ACROSS THE ROAD.

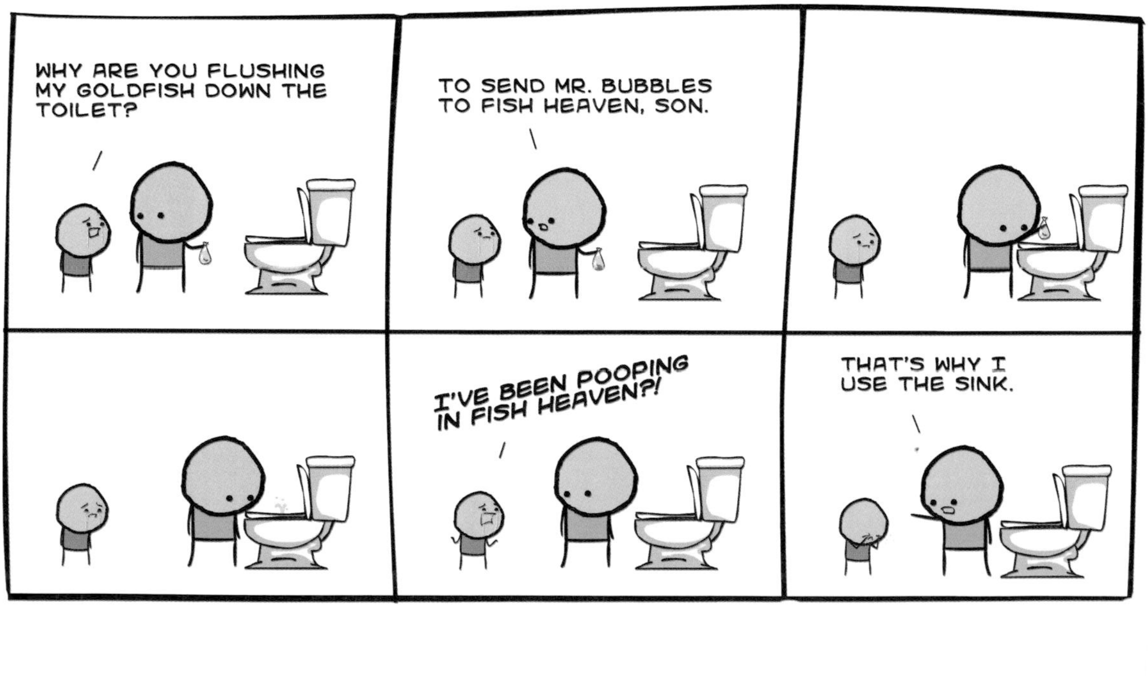
WHY ARE YOU FLUSHING MY GOLDFISH DOWN THE TOILET?
TO SEND MR. BUBBLES TO FISH HEAVEN, SON.
I'VE BEEN POOPING IN FISH HEAVEN?!
THAT'S WHY I USE THE SINK.

The Grabby Mitts of Death

You bought your innocuous infant an aquatic companion as a peer, since right now they seem to share the same brain. It made sense at the beginning—surely they'll find a bond in their shared interests of eating one type of food, staring into the mirror for long periods of time, and defecating all over their preferred environment? Alas, the fish hit the finish line first—you find him upside down one morning with no eyes, deader than James Dean's balls. "Time to put him in toilet," you say to your mourning child.

As you flush the fish unceremoniously down the bog like a sushi poop, your child asks if their dearly departed will find his way to Heaven from here. "Sure will," you chirp without a second thought, like a thoughtless finch. "So that's the way to Heaven, then?" Your child is starting to ask too much. You slit the throat of their line of thinking like a ninja with one simple response: "Yes." That'll get them out of your hair.

Big mistake. Now you are forced to cram every pet that you get into the toilet once they die, to ensure their safe passage through the pearly gates. Dogs. Cats. A long-tailed little monkey. Granny. You keep up the pretense with the foreboding sense that, once you eventually hit the eternal hay yourself, you'll be similarly whisked into the all-consuming toilet with all the dignity of a burp in the wind. Even dog shit gets buried in the garden. Every time you go to the bathroom, you stare into your own pre-dug grave. Then either piss or shit into it. You are contributing to your own inelegant passing every day.

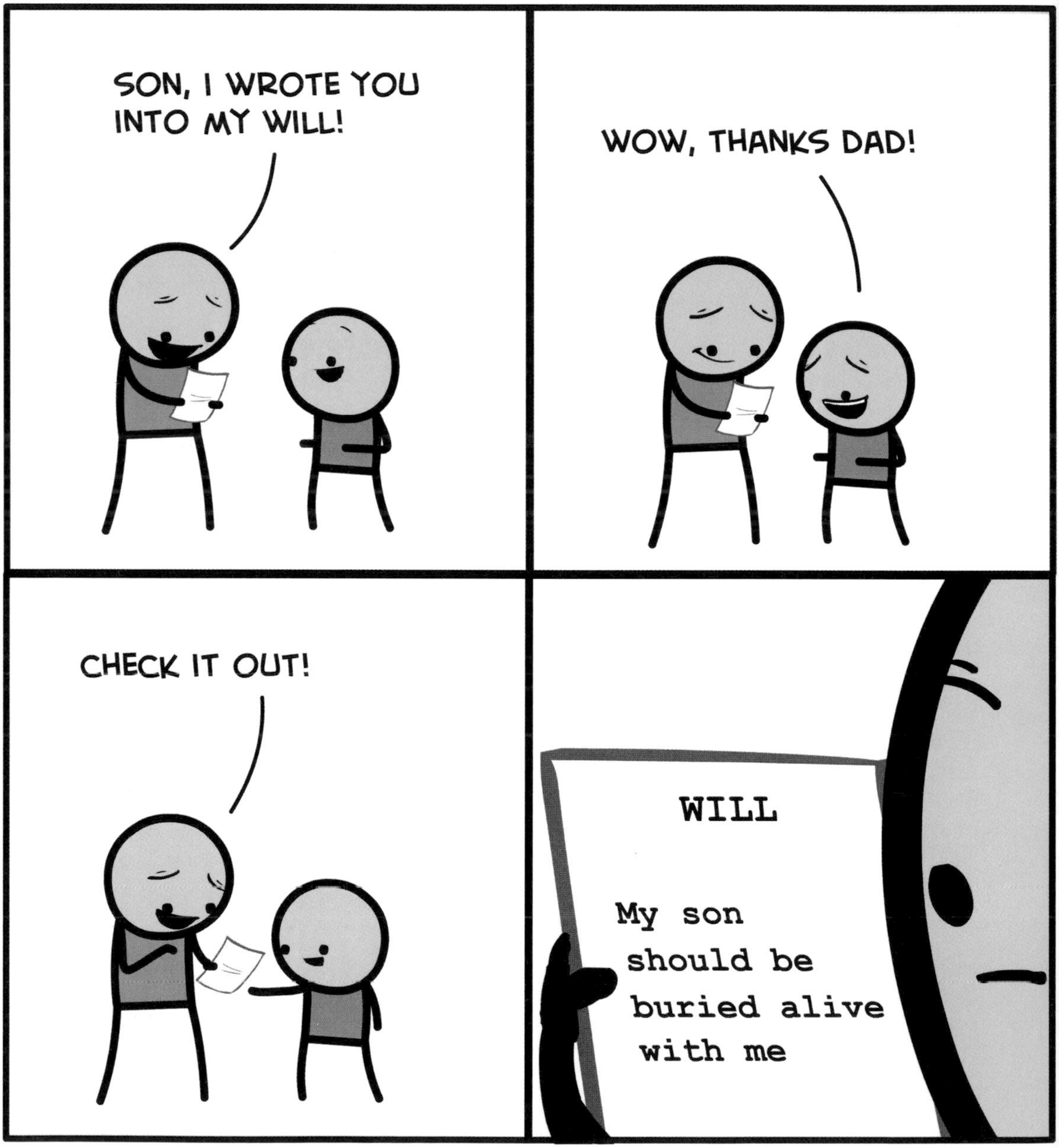
SON, I WROTE YOU INTO MY WILL!
WOW, THANKS DAD!
CHECK IT OUT!
WILL
My son should be buried alive with me

FIN . . . ?

You're on your bed of doom, making your last few people-noises. Your blurry sight conveys a family that has long privately prepared for this moment and is now already over it, waving you off enthusiastically as you embark on the unstoppable train ride to Deadsville. They prattle over any shared memories of you they can justify as good ones, all within the radar space of your croaking cochleae. "Hey, I can hear you!" the fading voice in your head moans. They've made it quite clear that it's your move. It's time to check your own mate. They anticipate your death with all the concern and slight impatience of waiting for a wi-fi router to restart. Just die already, and let us all get on with our lives. Me included.

You've still got one card up your gown, though. You beckon for your child to come close to your eroded, sand dune of a mouth, for you have one last nugget to pass down. "What is it, dear Papa?! Give me the shakedown, dead man!" your child whispers intimately to you. You reveal that you have nothing to give them other than financial ruin. Your coffin is the lost ark. Should they crack it open like a present on Christmas morning, they'll find nothing but destitution— but fear not, for you've arranged a solution.

You tell your child you've arranged for them to be buried with you, like a cat to your King Tutankhamun. You quip a small, timely joke about "toot and come in," because your child is about to come join you in the ground for all eternity.

Your facial expression changes from half-mustered cheeriness to deadly seriousness. Your child chuckles at your attempt at joviality, reveling in the small respite before taking in the full expanse of what you've just said. Suddenly, your candor washes over them like a cold bucket of water. They pause, searching for any hint that you aren't serious. They call it in after a few seconds, their brief expedition failed.

They stare deep into your eyes, their blood now starting to curdle. They stammer in a quiet breath, "You're . . . you're scaring me."

FATHER! I HEADED OVER AS SOON AS I HEARD THE NEWS!
COME CLOSER, SON... I HAVE ONE FINAL LESSON TO TEACH YOU BEFORE I DIE.
CLOSER...
CLOSER...
I'M CONTAGIOUS.

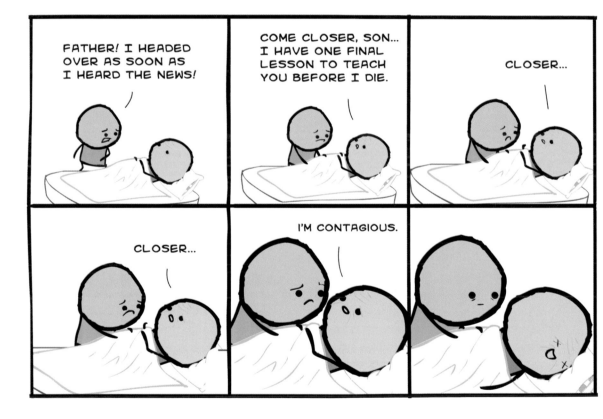

FIN.

You stare back, stoic and sterile as your child attempts to absorb your meaning. Their eyes widen to take in the gravity of this sinister, time-stopped moment, dark and sullen like a black hole.

Suddenly, you crack into a big smile like a new, sunny box of cornflakes. You laugh heartily, the loudest noise you've made in well over a week. "Joking!" you caw, still chuckling. Your child immediately jumps into your pool of alleviation, soaking in it. Washing the grime of the previous discomfort off their psyche. They laugh a big laugh. Still a little nervous, but hearty. They mimic the timing of your guffaws in an empathetic fashion.

Your family, half listening previously, halts their mutters, jumping at your unexpected expression of vigor. All heads are turned to you, awaiting what the noise means in all of its forms. Is this the rattle of death, or a sound you made cognizant, the final words of your script? They watch your intimate moment with your child as if staring into a snow globe, peering in, to watch the moment unfurl as organically as can be. Two relatives hold each other. Another's lip shakes from witnessing the delicacy of your base, primal interactions. The frailness of life is on full display. Everyone in the room is reminded of the impermanence of their flesh.

Your laughs segue into desperate gasps, your expression changing from cheery to frightened. You reach a hand up around your neck to wrench some control over your internal commotion. The chaos echoes across the room as your family slowly joins in on your brouhaha, muttering and panicking. You leap forward and let out one final cough – qwaf! – covering your child's face in phlegm, before ultimately limping back into your pillow.

(Continued on next page)

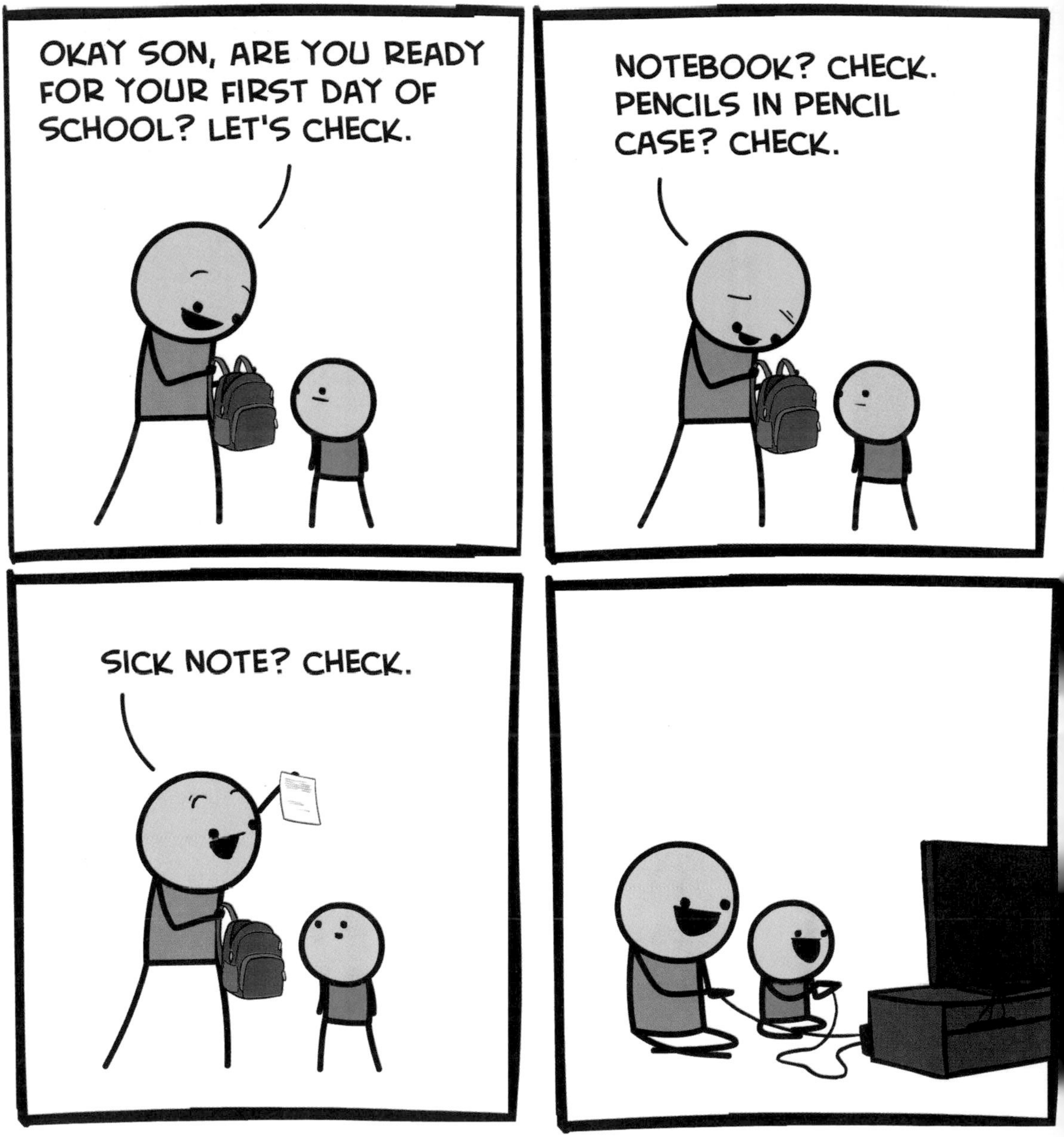
OKAY SON, ARE YOU READY FOR YOUR FIRST DAY OF SCHOOL? LET'S CHECK.
NOTEBOOK? CHECK. PENCILS IN PENCIL CASE? CHECK.
SICK NOTE? CHECK.

The room comes to rest. You lie motionless, gone. The clan brings their hands up to their mouths, finally having borne witness to the horrible main event of this gathering, still unprepared for the promptness of your exit. Your life didn't close itself down carefully like some Terminator GUI. It just shut off in a flash. No white light or pearly gate. Your child slowly wipes your mucus off their own face, looking down in their hands at the last remnant of your living body to have graced them physically. Curtains are drawn. People are hustled. Blankets are pulled.

The following day, your child develops a disturbing cough of their own. Ambulances quickly arrive. Brouhaha is roused once again after having barely slept from yesterday. By the time they arrive at the hospital, they have already passed on. "Cerebrospinal meningitis, sudden onset. Probably caught contagiously," mutters the doctor after a couple of quick tests.

You've got the little bastard now. You weren't joking at all.

You and your child play Mario World in Heaven as both of your corpses are hastily stuffed into your coffin like two bratwursts in a toilet roll, having finally escaped from the morose marathon that is life.

FIN! (For Real)

Here's you and your kid playing video games for all eternity, joyfully. The schoolbag represents life, the sick note the literal sick notes you were hitting as you hacked phlegm all over your child's face. There. There's your happy ending. Now get out of here.*

*Don't try any of this book at home.

Special Thanks to
Kate McElfatrick

Additional Thanks to
Jasmine Amiri

Designer
Scott Newman

Assistant Editor
Katalina Holland

Editor
Bryce Carlson

CYANIDE & HAPPINESS: A Guide to Parenting by Three Guys With No Kids, October 2018. Published by BOOM! Studios, a division of Boom Entertainment, Inc.

For other Cyanide & Happiness comics, animated shorts, books, and merchandise, visit www.explosm.net

For information regarding the CPSIA on this printed material, call: (203) 595-3636 and provide reference #RICH – 821025.

BOOM! Studios, 5670 Wilshire Boulevard, Suite 400, Los Angeles, CA 90036-5679. Printed in USA. Second Printing.

ISBN: 978-1-68415-002-1, eISBN: 978-1-61398-673-8